GOD'S MESSAGE TO THE CHRISTIAN CHURCH

Back to the Roots of the Christian Faith

Rev. W. Lewis Autrey and Robert S. Autrey

Published by
Innovo Publishing, LLC
www.innovopublishing.com
1-888-546-2111

Providing Full-Service Publishing Services for
Christian Authors, Artists & Organizations: Hardbacks, Paperbacks,
eBooks, Audiobooks, Music & Videos

God's Message to the Christian Church: Back to the Roots of the Christian Faith
Copyright © 2012 by W. Lewis Autrey
All rights reserved.

No part of this publication may be reproduced, stored in a retrieval system,
or transmitted in any form or by any means electronic, mechanical,
photocopying, recording, or otherwise, without the prior
written permission of the author.

Unless otherwise indicated, Scripture is taken from the *Holy Bible, New Living Translation*, Copyright
©1996. Used by permission of Tyndale House Publishers, Inc.,
Carol Stream, Illinois, 60188. All rights reserved.

Scripture marked NTME is taken from *The New Testament in Modern English* (Revised).
Copyright ©J. B. Phillips 1958, 1960, 1972. New York: Simon & Schuster.

Scripture marked KJV is taken from *The Holy Bible: Authorized King James Version*. Copyright ©1986.
Iowa Falls: World Bible Publishers, Inc.

Scripture marked NIV is taken from The Holy Bible: New International Version Giant Print
Reference Bible, Copyright ©1990 by the Zondervan Corporation. All rights reserved.

Library of Congress Control Number 2012931659
ISBN 13: 978-1-936076-85-7

Cover Design & Interior Layout: Innovo Publishing, LLC

Printed in the United States of America
U.S. Printing History

First Edition: February 2012

Dedicated to the loving memory of my father,

the late Rev. W. C. Autrey (1913–1989),
who died before God began to give me
the revelation and inspiration necessary to write this book.
Yet, I know he is watching, along with all of the other great saints
(Abraham, Isaac, Jacob, etc.) to see if I will finish the work God has chosen
for me to do. I know I will see him again when Christ returns.

ACKNOWLEDGMENTS

I want to thank my loving wife, Joyce E. Autrey; my daughter, April Autrey; my son, Lewis C. Autrey; and my son, Robert S. Autrey, for all the time and energy they spent in assisting me with research and for giving me inspiration to write this book. They didn't realize it, but it was their patience and kindness that gave me the inspiration to keep going. Every writer needs encouragement from time to time. And I thank God for inspiring the people I love to be an inspiration to me.

I pray that God's mercy and kindness will continue to shine upon my wife and family until the great day of the Lord's return. Then, at that time, we will all meet the Lord in the air and be with Him forever.

FOREWORD

The American Christian Church has drifted far away from the truth and knowledge of Christ over the last five or six decades. For the most part, this wandering away was not done to intentionally deceive or defy God. Still, Satan has inspired many well-meaning theologians to sincerely believe and teach that this drifting away is just a new and better understanding of what God wanted for us all along. Consequently, the church of God is left in total and complete confusion about its true destiny.

The words of Jesus have been forgotten, and instead, the dreams and inspirations of people [our preachers] have been substituted in their place. God never intended for it to be this way, but He did predict that it would happen [Matthew 24]. He plainly warned us that many would turn away from the true faith and that the love of many [toward God and their fellowman] would grow cold. He even said that Satan would so deceive the world that the entire human race would be in danger of being destroyed [going to hell]. But He also told us that for the elect's sake [those who are called to salvation] He will not allow this to happen.

The purpose of writing this book, then, is to remind God's people of Jesus' own words [actual words] and their intended meanings. And whenever possible, instead of giving my personal opinion, I will allow Jesus, Himself, to tell us what His will is for us. And as always, you should confirm everything by opening up your Bible and checking the word of God. Hopefully, in this way we will be taken back to the roots of our Christian faith, the purity of the Gospel of Christ, and Christ Himself, without whom there would be no Christian faith. Then we can better appreciate what Christ has done for us and the wonderful destiny that awaits us in heaven.

CONTENTS

Introduction: Before The Foundation Of The World 9

Part 1: What Is The Gospel? 13
   1 - In The Day You Eat Thereof 19
   2 - Redemption 23
   3 - Forgiveness Of Sins 25
   4 - Some Words Of Jesus To His Saints 31
   5 - Christian Baptism And The Trumpets 37
   6 - Why The Cross? 43

Part 2: God As The Christ 53
   7 - Jesus The Christ 55
   8 - Is Jesus God? 61
   9 - Christ In Ezekiel's Wheel 73
   10 - Complete In Christ: The Final Blessing 79

Part 3: Living Forever In Christ 87
   11 - Eternal Life 89
   12 - Heaven: The New Garden Of Eden 97

Part 4: Christ Is The Way! 105
   13 - Why God Gave Us The Law 107
   14 - The Biblical Meaning Of Tithing 113
   15 - Who Is The Beast? 119
   16 - Satan: The Abomination Of Desolation 125
   17 - Blasphemy Against The Holy Spirit 131

Part 5: Belonging To Christ 135
   18 - The Choice Is Ours: Keep Believing 137
   19 - The Rapture 143
   20 - God Is Spirit 147

Epilogue: A Final Word To The Church 151

INTRODUCTION:
BEFORE THE FOUNDATION OF THE WORLD

We can all be thankful to God for sending Christ into the world. This proves that God loves us more than we can ever know. This love is so great that if thousands of books were written on the subject, they would hardly make a dent into its importance. But we have what we need to know about it in the Scriptures.

Paul stated in 1 Corinthians 2:1–8, *"Dear brothers and sisters, when I first came to you I didn't use lofty words and brilliant ideas to tell you God's message. . . . No, the wisdom we speak of is the secret wisdom of God, which was hidden in the former times, though he made it for our benefit before the world began. But the rulers of this world have not understood it . . ."*

Paul further stated:

He is so rich in kindness that he purchased our freedom through the blood of his Son, and our sins are forgiven. He has showered his kindness on us, along with all wisdom and understanding.
God's secret plan has now been revealed to us; it is a plan centered on Christ, designed long ago according to his good pleasure. And this is his plan: At the right time he will bring everything together under the authority of Christ—everything in heaven and on earth. Furthermore, because of Christ, we have received an inheritance from God, for he chose us from the beginning, and all things happen just as he decided long ago.

> *God's purpose was that we who were the first to trust in Christ should praise our glorious God. And now you also have heard the truth, the Good news that God saves you. And when you believed in Christ, he identified you as his own by giving you the Holy Spirit, whom he promised long ago. The Spirit is God's guarantee that he will give us everything he promised and that he has purchased us to be his own people. This is just one more reason for us to praise our glorious God* (Ephesians 1:7–14).

Specifically, then, God's plan was to send Jesus to die in the place of all men, regardless of what sins they committed or whether they are Jews or Gentiles (whether or not they lived under the law) (Romans 3:9). Thus, we read in 2 Corinthians 5:14–15, *"Whatever we do, it is because Christ's love controls us. Since we believe that Christ died for everyone, we also believe that we have all died to the old life we used to live. He died for everyone so that those who receive his new life will no longer live to please themselves. Instead, they will live to please Christ, who died and was raised for them."*

Paul said to Timothy (1 Timothy 4:9–11), *"This is true, and everyone should accept it. We work hard and suffer much in order that people will believe the truth, for our hope is in the living God, who is the Savior of all people, particularly of those who believe. Teach these things and insist that everyone learn them."*

The crucifixion account of Jesus is true. That is, the evidence of Christ's horrible and painful death is unquestioned by those who believe. Look at the record for yourself. Even with all the pain, Jesus thought of us rather than Himself. His first words from the cross were, *"Father, forgive these people, because they don't know what they are doing"* (Luke 23:34).

All we have to do to escape the death our sins have brought upon us is to accept that Jesus died in our place!

But some may ask, "How does God plan to save us from death after we have already died?" The answer is: God deals with this problem by raising us from the dead on the last day (John 6:44). According to Romans 3:24, since we believe in Christ we have been declared by God not guilty of any sins worthy of death. This is what Jesus meant when He said that those who believe in Him will never die (John 6:58).

"I am the resurrection and the life," Jesus told Martha. *"Those who believe in me, even though they die like everyone else, will live again. They are given eternal life for believing in me and will never perish [die]. Do you believe this, Martha?"* (John 11:25–26) He told the Jews, *"Don't be so surprised! Indeed, the time is coming when all the dead in their graves will hear the voice of God's Son, and they will rise again. Those who have done good will rise to eternal life, and those who have continued in evil will rise to judgment"* (John 5:28–29).

But in the case of people who do not accept Christ as their substitute, God has a different plan. According to the Bible, any person in this situation dies, just as anyone else does. Only now, he is not raised to eternal life, (1 Corinthians 15:20), but to eternal destruction and damnation (Daniel 12:2; Mark 9:48). Eternal life is reserved only for those who have accepted Christ.

Daniel says it this way:

At that time Michael, the archangel who stands guard over your nation, will rise. Then there will be a time of anguish greater than any since nations first came into existence. But at that time every one of your people whose name is written in the book will be rescued. Many of those whose bodies lie dead and buried will rise up, some to everlasting life and some to shame and everlasting contempt. Those who are wise will shine as bright as they sky, and those who turn many to righteousness will shine like stars forever (Daniel 12:2–3).

We must take God at His word. This is why we must believe the warning given to us in the book of Acts and repent of our sins: *"God overlooked people's former ignorance about these things, but now he commands everyone everywhere to turn away from idols and turn to him. For he has set a day for judging the world with justice by the man he has appointed (Christ), and he proved to everyone who this is by raising him from the dead"* (Acts 17:30–31).

But in order for us to explain God's plan to others, we must have knowledge of the plan itself, and not be confused when we hear of counterfeit plans. Then, too, we must know that Satan, God's arch enemy, will always try to prevent us from gaining the things God has in store for us.

May God guide our reading!

PART 1
WHAT IS THE GOSPEL?

1
IN THE DAY YOU EAT THEREOF

The Bible reveals that what we call life today is actually a state of death, imposed upon the human race because of the sins of Adam. That man is in a state of death is seen by what we read in 1 John 3:14: *"If we love our Christian brothers and sisters, it proves that we have passed from death to eternal life. But a person who has no love is still dead."* Romans 8:10 reads: *"And Christ lives within in you, so even though your body will die because of sin, the Spirit gives you life because you have been made right with God."*

These Scriptures are easy to understand. I wonder how we missed them. But now that we know about them, God will not be pleased with us if we ignore what is plainly taught and continue in our old ways. God wants us to learn as much as we can about His plan of salvation and teach it to others. This way, we show Him that we are truly His disciples.

About our state of death, John MacArthur comments, "When Adam sinned, he brought death on himself and everybody else. . . . We all inherit what I like to call the death force. . . . And we battle all through life to keep the death force from being triumphant for as long as we can. We not only inherit death, we inherit sin, because we were all there in Adam. . . . When Adam sinned, everybody sinned in Adam. And when Adam received the penalty of death, we were all sentenced to die. . . ."[1]

Reverend E. V. Hill comments, "There was a time when Adam was alive both physically and spiritually. But sin entered the world, and our spirits and souls died. Only God's spirit can make our spirits and souls alive again. Only He can give us the ability to worship Him or communicate with Him."[2]

Ephesians 2:1–7 says:

Once you were dead.... You used to live just like the rest of the world, full of sin, obeying Satan, the mighty prince of the power of the air....

But God is so rich in mercy, and he loved us so much, that even while we were dead because of our sins, he gave us life when he raised Christ from the dead.... [God] ... raised us from the dead along with Christ, and we are seated with him in the heavenly realms—all because we are one with Christ Jesus. And so God can always point to us as examples of the incredible wealth of his favor and kindness toward us, as shown in all he has done for us through Christ Jesus.

Why would Paul make this statement if it were not true? God called Paul for a special mission—to take the Gospel to the Gentile world. This mission involved coming in contact with all types of theories and philosophies. Gentiles, then, would have been familiar with the concepts of the meaning of life. When Paul explained to them that they didn't have life apart from Jesus, they could see his logic, even though they might not have agreed with it.

They had gods such as Zeus, Apollo, Hermes, and Artemis. These gods claimed to be their makers and sustainers. The Greek-speaking people looked to them for life. But the problem was they thought they were already alive. And this is still the problem today. People are doing all the things they want to do, and they think that they are alive. But they don't understand that the reason they are still walking around is because God is merciful and is all powerful. He does this to give them time to repent.

Then when we read these Scriptures from the Bible people get upset. They think we are trying to make them unhappy. They say we are depressing them. The Gospel is not depressing; it is the way to eternal life.

That God took the life of Adam that day, there is no doubt. Even civil authorities have the right to take the life of people who disobey. God gave the civil authorities of Moses' day the right to put to death anyone who blasphemed the name of God or killed another person (Leviticus 24:16–17). In Exodus 21:17, He gave them the right to execute people who cursed their parents. God even gave the Romans the right to execute His own Son, Jesus Christ (John 19:11).

This is what the Gospel is all about. The most famous verse in the Bible, John 3:16, speaks about the possibility of us living again. It plainly states that if we believe in Jesus, He will give us life. Ask yourself, is this true? Will He really give me life? Will He really place me in a position that enables me to live again? If the answers to these questions is yes, then what are we waiting for? Let's look to Jesus for life.

God did not send Jesus into the world to condemn us. God did not send Jesus into the world to keep us in our old state of being either. He wants us to live. Have you ever wondered why God speaks of Himself as the living God as opposed to the dead God? He is making a point. The point is He is alive, and He wants us to be alive so we can be with Him. The living doesn't associate with the dead.

Sin kills. Sin takes life. This is the theme all through the Bible, from Genesis to Revelation. So Paul is stressing this same theme. Once you were dead because of your sins. At that time, you lived for Satan. In fact, Satan is the one who caused your death. In this state, you lived any way you wanted to. You didn't care because you didn't know God. But now that you know God, Christ has placed His Spirit in you and has given you life. And this is not just any life; this is eternal life. Yes, this is God's incredible gift to you. This is God's special favor.

That Jesus would come all the way from heaven and offer us this gift is amazing. He didn't have to do this, you know. It's not as if He was forced to. He did this of His own free will, a testimony to His great love for us. He did this because we are His special creation, His pride and joy. Why this is so, I don't know, but it is. That's what so amazing about the Bible; it presents to us things about God that we would otherwise not know. *"That is what the Scriptures mean when they say, 'No eye has seen, no ear has heard, and no mind has imagined what God has prepared for those who love him'"* (1 Corinthians 2:9).

Just think about it. If you are in Christ, your spirit is now alive and will always be. This is a comforting thought. And though your body is still dead, God will bring it alive on the last day. This will be done by giving you a new live body to match your live spirit. This will happen not only to you but to all who believe in Jesus and look forward to His coming.

If you are not in Christ, you can be. Do you want God to impart to you new life? Do you want to live with Jesus in heaven for all eternity? If so, please accept Jesus into your heart and pledge to live for Him. This will make Him your personal Savior. This will make Him your friend and comforter. This will make Him your Lord and Master, the One who looks after you in all your trials and tests. This will make Him the One who cares for you when no one else does. This will make Him the One you can count on when you come to the end of this earthly existence and pass into eternity.

Jesus stands at the door and knocks. Let's open our hearts to Him and let Him in. Let's stop rejecting Him the way our ancestor, Adam, did. Even though Adam and his wife were deceived, they still made the deliberate choice to sin. But we need not be deceived today, nor do we have to make the choice to remain in sin. We have the record of what happened plainly laid out for us in the Scriptures. This is the word of God. This is the word of Jesus. Let's take Jesus at His word, repent of our sins, and turn to Him for life.

This state of death the unsaved are in is nothing to take lightly. It can only end one way. Jesus compared it to dead grass that is plucked up and burned at harvest time. Do you see the point? Dead things are good for nothing, except to be thrown into the fire, i.e., the fires of hell. You don't want to end up this way.

But Jesus is always there to help us. He is always there to feed us. He feeds us with His word, and He gives us His Spirit to help us understand His word. Let us always be faithful and read God's instructions—the Holy Bible—to us. Here, we will find everything we need to find life. And as a bonus, the Holy Spirit will inspire us to keep on learning. Then we will truly be growing in grace and the knowledge of our Lord Jesus Christ.

May God keep you always!

---

1. "... Sin ... —John MacArthur," pp. 1–11 <http:www.biblebb.com/files/MAC/90-233.htm>; Internet; accessed 19 August 2009.

2. E. V. Hill, *Victory in Jesus* (Chicago: Moody Press, 2003), 14.

2

REDEMPTION

The purpose of this chapter is to explain the role of redemption in the lives of God's people. And as we do this, we will focus primarily on Jesus, the great redeemer, who pardons us from our sins and restores us to the right relationship with Him.

We see redemption mentioned in Psalm 34:21–22: *"Calamity will surely overtake the wicked, and those who hate the righteous will be punished. But the* LORD *will redeem those who serve him. Everyone who trusts in him will be freely pardoned."* Psalm 19:13–14 states: *"Keep me from deliberate sins! Don't let them control me. Then I will be free of guilt and innocent of great sin. May the words of my mouth and the thoughts of my heart be pleasing to you, O Lord, my rock and my redeemer."*

The meaning, here, is that those who are in sin are doomed to destruction and are slaves to sin and Satan. As such, their only hope is to be bought back from sin. If they are not bought back or redeemed, they have no hope for life. The whole world is in this state. The whole world needs Jesus. That is why He is spoken of by David as "my rock," and then "my redeemer."

David knew this because God redeemed him. He committed many sins, including murder, adultery, and rebellion against God. But he repented and called out to God, and God saved him. This should serve as an example for us. We, too, must call out to God.

Psalm 49:7–8 reads: *"Yet they cannot redeem themselves from death by paying a ransom to God. Redemption does not come so easily, for no one can ever pay enough to live forever and never see the grave."* That is, we cannot buy redemption because this is not the price God has set. The price God set is the blood of His Son, Jesus.

The following two Scriptures make the point:

1. *"And she coming in that instant gave thanks likewise unto the Lord, and spake of him to all them that looked for redemption in Jerusalem"* (Luke 2:38, KJV).

2. *"In whom we have redemption through his blood, the forgiveness of sins, according to the riches of his grace;"* (Ephesians 1:7, KJV).

Ben Reaoch remarked:

To be redeemed is to be set free from bondage. What is it that binds us? What is it that holds us in slavery? What is it that keeps us from experiencing the joy of freedom? Of course, it's sin. Before redemption, before we are redeemed (set free), sin is our master. Sin rules over us and enslaves us, and it pervades our entire being. We are sinners through and through, in our nature, and in our actions, and in our attitudes. And there is a just punishment for being a sinner, as the next phrase implies, "the forgiveness of our trespasses." As sinners we are in bondage to sin. . . . But in Christ God sets . . . [men] free from the bondage to sin and He removes the punishment for sin. He redeems us and forgives us.[1]

As pointed out above: CHRIST REDEEMS US BY HIS BLOOD! But from the earliest of time, man has thought that he could redeem himself. That is the face and purpose of man's false religion. Satan inspired this evil, of course. We can recognize it by the list of rules it presents to us, and the list of disciplines it puts forth to replace Christ. These serve to uplift man as his own savior and lower Christ to a somewhat unimportant figure.

The fact that man wants to be uplifted is suggested by the way he exalts himself at every opportunity. He gives himself lofty titles, high and honorable platitudes of nobility, and even in religion, titles of honor that approach the reverence of God.

Remember what Satan said to Eve in the garden in Genesis 3:4: *"You won't die."* In other words, if you won't die, then, what need is there for Christ to die in your place? Yes, he will tell you early on that he will, but don't believe it. So if he does make reference to His death, just ignore it. It does not affect anything you do now or in the future. In fact, if you eat of this tree, you can be like God. What a lie!

We could translate Satan's lie like this: "You don't need a redeemer. By your new knowledge of things to come, you can save yourselves. Just trust in who you are. Just trust in the God within you. It is enough. You are a high and noble creature. You are high and honorable."

I have seen so many people with this kind of thinking. They walk around so sure of themselves and their abilities. It is as if they know everything there is to know about the here and now and the life to come. They say to themselves, "I have it made; I am a good person. And even if I am not, it is my business. What right does anyone have to tell me what to do? What business is it of theirs? Just look at the people around me. I am not half as bad as they are."

If man could save himself, there would not be all the trouble in the world that we see around us. Even at the writing of this book, there are wars and riots throughout the Middle East. The people are all in a state of unrest. Wars rage to overthrow unwanted dictators. Other dictators have abandoned their countries and fled for their lives. But I ask myself, "What will be the end of all of this. Will it all turn out for good? Or are we just seeing the first stages of another lethal round of trouble?" I option for the latter.

Also, we worry about global warming and if the world will become too warm to sustain human life. In some places, sustained drought has caused water shortages that threaten our ability to grow food. Some areas of the world suffer from too much water, that is, too much rain producing floods. This has washed away topsoil and the soil protecting vegetation at an alarming rate. Other areas suffer from the effects of crop-destroying insects. What can we do?

But listen to what is written is Isaiah 12 1–4: *"Praise the LORD! He was angry with me, but now he comforts me. See, God has come to save me. I will trust in him and not be afraid. The LORD God is my strength and my song; he has become my salvation.'*

'With joy you will drink deeply from the fountain of salvation! In that wonderful day, you will sing: 'Thank the LORD. Praise his name. . . .'"

Isaiah could say this because he saw God (Jesus) in a magnificent vision. God was sitting on a throne in splendid glory. The train of His robe was so all-encompassing it filled the Temple. Hovering around Him were many mighty angelic beings called seraphim. Each had six wings: two wings to cover their faces, two wings to cover their feet, and two wings to enable them to fly.

In one mighty voice they sang, *"Holy, holy, holy is the Lord God almighty. The whole earth is filled with his glory!"* (Isaiah 6:3). This mighty shout shot through the whole Temple, giving God even more glory. In addition, the Temple was filled with smoke. I can just imagine the other angels looking on. They must have longed to be a part of this singing group. And they must have asked God to allow them to do so. But He had other duties for them.

Then Isaiah shouted, *"My destruction is sealed, for I am a sinful man and a member of a sinful race . . . "* (Isaiah 6:5). This is something many of us should realize.

But an amazing thing happened. One of the seraphim went over to the altar and picked up a burning coal with a pair of tongs. He touched this coal to Isaiah's lips and announced that his guilt was removed.

Apparently, this angel had foreknowledge. He too knew the prophecies scattered through the Old Testament about the coming redeemer. That is, the One sitting on the throne is the One who would become our burning coal, and would burn away our guilt. Isaiah didn't argue with the seraphim because he knew he was right. This fact had been revealed to Isaiah too.

This Jesus came to earth as a lowly human being. He gave up His glory and refused to be exalted. He was born in the lowest possible place, a lowly stable in one of the smallest villages in Judea. He was so poor His mother had to wrap him in rags and lay Him in a manger. Surrounded by His parents, He spent His first night on earth with the cattle. He took the lowest seat and ate with common people. And not once did He neglect them.

I thank God we have been privileged to this great news by the preaching of the Gospel. And what a privilege it is to live at a time when this great news is being preached. Think about it; there were times when we could not say this. In Isaiah's day, for instance, the Gospel was limited to the prophets and to the few God allowed them to come in contact with.

But even then, most people wouldn't listen. They told Isaiah to shut up and stop preaching about this coming redeemer. *"We don't want any more of your reports." "Don't tell us the truth. Tell us nice things. Tell us lies. Forget all this gloom. We have heard more than enough about your 'Holy One of Israel'"* (Isaiah 30:10–11).

Can you imagine that? Seven hundred years before the birth of Christ people were saying the very thing we hear so much of today. People may not use these exact same words, but the intent is the same. And people are just as obstinate.

But God's answer is: because you won't listen, calamity will come upon you. And it will not be the type of calamity you think; it will be the calamity of hell's fires where there will be weeping and gnashing of teeth. In verses 12–14 He used the metaphoric words, *"Because you despise what I tell you and trust instead in oppression and lies, calamity will come upon you suddenly. It will be like a bulging wall that bursts and falls. In an instant, it will collapse and come crashing down. You will be smashed like a piece of pottery—shattered so completely that there won't be a piece left that is big enough to carry coals from a fireplace or a little water from the well."*

Yet, people don't care. Instead, they flock to Eastern religions. Others flock to fun and frolic and other types of escapism. They fade off into a make-believe world where everything ends happily. The trouble is that everything does not end happily in the real world. In the real world, the devil is not obligated to abide by anything we say or think. The Bible calls him the "god of this world." In other words, he is the one who says what he intends to do, not us.

I am not saying that the devil is more powerful than God. He is not. But he does operate within the limits God has set for him, and they are vast. It has to be this way because Adam turned over his legal authority to the devil when he disobeyed God. This relieved God of any obligation to ward off Satan and his attacks upon man. But God does intervene on our behalf when it suits His purpose, i.e., when it is according to His will.

But let's get back to the basics of redemption. When the law demanded our lives because of our sins, Jesus, our advocate, went to the Judge (God), and said, "I will die in their place, Your Honor. Count me as guilty and count them as not guilty."

God honored this request and placed the sins of the world upon Jesus. He placed not only the sins of the righteous, but the sins of the unrighteous upon Him too. But the catch is you must accept this glorious act of redemption for it to be effective in your life. But most people are not willing to do this. They just do not see themselves guilty of anything, and therefore, do not want to repent. This makes them a rebel with Satan, unwilling to escape from his confinement and prison.

I see people every day who are this way. They are so cool to what we say about Jesus. When we come by, they turn their backs and look the other way. Some make up stories in an effort to stop us from trying to convert them. One preacher tells of passing out eight hundred flyers in a local community, and on the morning of the crusade, not one person bothered to show up. Some drove by and didn't even bother to look over.

Let's conclude this way. On a hill outside Jerusalem, two thousand years ago, our Savior was placed on a cross between two thieves. It was not for crimes He had committed. He was innocent. He had done no wrong. He WENT THERE AS OUR REDEEMER. That is, by His death, He bought back the whole of mankind. All we have to do is believe that this took place and believe that it applies to our lives. Then we can be saved and have a home in heaven.

All praised to Him who loves us!

---

1 ". . . Redeemed through Christ's Blood . . .," pp. 1–6 http://www.3riversgrace.org/sermons/manuscript/Eph_1B.pdf; Internet; accessed 3 July 2006.

3

FORGIVENESS OF SINS

Jesus told His us in Matthew 6:14 that if we forgive those who sin against us, our heavenly Father will forgive us when we sin against Him. But this raises the question: Why do sins need to be forgiven, and on what basis does God grant us forgiveness? And why are those who are forgiven now on a sound basis with God?

We need our sins forgiven because God hates sin. He cannot stand to look at it. Sin is totally against God's pure and undefiled nature. Unconfessed sin comes between us and God, damaging the relationship. That is, it places the sinner under the condemnation of punishment, and it forces God to punish the sinner. *"When I refused to confess my sin, I was weak and miserable, and I groaned all day long. Day and night your hand of discipline was heavy on me. My strength evaporated like water in the summer heat. Interlude"* (Psalm 32:3–4).

Think of it like this. If God did not punish sin, sin could not be declared as evil. It would be just another alternative lifestyle—just another way of expressing one's point of view. Then the rebellion of mankind would be looked upon as being just as right as God, and not God's enemy, and there would be no need to preach about the dangers of sin.

God deals with those who repent through the act of forgiveness— He remits or removes the trespass of sin, as well as annuls or removes sin's penalties. Forgiveness removes the guilt of the guilty and withdraws the displeasure of the offended. Colossians 2:14 describes forgiveness as the cancelling of *"the record that contained the charges against us."* Ephesians 4:32 describes forgiveness as the way God displays His *"tenderhearted"* compassion.

The legal basis for God's forgiveness is the cross of Christ—Christ's blood washes away our sins. *"And from Jesus Christ, who is the faithful witness, and the first begotten of the dead, and the prince of the kings of the earth. [And] unto him that loved us, and washed us from our sins in his own blood"* (Revelation 1:5, KJV). *"Then he adds, 'I will never again remember their sins and lawless deeds.' Now when sins have been forgiven, there is no need to offer any more sacrifices"* (Hebrews 10:17–18). Now, we can be as clean and pure as snow!

The price God paid for us was high—the death of His only Son. Imagine how this must have grieved Him. Imagine further how He must have felt when He saw us disobeying Him by submitting ourselves to Satan. Then imagine even further how He must have felt when He saw the misery and destruction it brought upon us. Yet, because of His great love, He purified and washed us clean BY FORGIVING OUR SINS based on His atoning death!

Listed below are three Scriptures that prove God forgives our sins:

1. "Forgive the rebellious sins of my youth; look instead through the eyes of your . . . love. . . ." (Psalm 25:7).
2. "He has removed our rebellious acts as far away from us as the east is from the west" (Psalm 103:12).
3. "[And] . . . forgive us our sins, just as we have forgiven those who have sinned against us" (Matthew 6:12).

Now let's address the need for God's forgiveness in more detail. If only a few of us needed to be forgiven, God could simply write us off and save the remainder. But this is not possible, since all of us need God's forgiveness. This puts God in the position of making salvation available to all of us, or none of us.

In addition, the whole universe is looking at God's response to the problem. Specifically, Satan and his demons are watching. They wonder that since God did not forgive them, how He can now forgive humans. To them, the whole thing does not make sense. Their response is to try to destroy the plan. The holy angels, too, are watching God's response. But their response is different. They understand they would have never sacrificed themselves for us, but they wonder what is prompting God to do it. They are just as anxious as anyone to see the outcome.

Even God's very own people have trepidations about this subject. They know from reading the Law of Moses that it is a sin to lie, steal, cheat, murder, etc. The law tells them that people who do such things should be punished. The criminal court system, the police force, the military, heads of state, kings and queens, and even some parents punish offenders. So why doesn't God?

The answer: God is not in the killing business. He wants to see as many people as possible saved (1 Timothy 2:4). Accordingly, He chooses to forgive! It could be said that God chooses to save rather than destroy, to "let live" rather than to "let die," and to love rather than hate.

David wrote this about God's unfailing love for us:

> *Your unfailing love, O L*ORD*, is as vast as the heavens; your faithfulness reaches beyond the clouds. Your righteousness is like the mighty mountains, your justice like the ocean depths. You care for people . . . O L*ORD*. How precious is your unfailing love, O God! All humanity finds shelter in the shadow of your wings. You feed them from the abundance of your house, letting them drink from your rivers of delight. [Truly,] . . . you are the fountain of life, the light by which we see* (Psalm 36:5–9).

Psalm 48:9–11 records: *"O God, we meditate on your unfailing love as we worship in your Temple. As your name deserves, O God, you will be praised to the ends of the earth. Your strong right hand is filled with victory. Let the people on Mount Zion rejoice. Let the towns of Judah be glad, for your judgments are just."*

The world's unsaved have doubts too. They don't even believe in God's love. And they rarely forgive each other. This is especially true of people they don't like. If they don't like you, you are in for a long, hard ride. And you won't like where this ride will take you. Often it ends in disaster, either for you, or for someone else. Stories are often told of people taking their unforgiveness to the grave. Other stories are told of people passing their hard feelings on from generation to generation. Even whole countries are caught up in their cycle, making for perilous results.

And don't forget about the people of other religions. They look at us and wonder what is going on. "How can we teach forgiveness," they say. "The gods of our religion don't forgive us. We have to work our way into heaven, and if our good deeds don't outweigh our bad deeds, we don't make it."

But our forgiveness is the reason Jesus went to the cross. His words: *"Father, forgive these people, because they don't know what they are doing"* (Luke 23:34) are a reminder of this very fact. He knew that His death would make it possible for the world to be reconciled to God!

> *[Amen,] all this newness of life is from God, who brought us back to himself through what Christ did. And God has given us the task of reconciling people to him. For God was in Christ, reconciling the world to himself, no longer counting people's sins against them. This is the wonderful message he has given us to tell others. We are Christ's ambassadors, and God is using us to speak to you. We urge you, as though Christ himself were here pleading with you. "Be reconciled*

to God!" For God made Christ, who never sinned, to be the offering for our sin, so that we could be made right with God through Christ* (2 Corinthians 5:18–21).

In forgiveness, then, a dirty sinner is made not only to feel clean, but in God's sight, to actually be clean. The sinner is now one of God's cleansed children. All of heaven is filled with joy when this takes place! This puts us in a new relationship with Him, and disarms all accusers and doubters.

One cannot buy forgiveness though! If we could, what chance would the people have who are extremely poor? And what about the people who live in an economy that does not use money, or have very little use for it? Undoubtedly, they would be left out of God's love. We must be careful, therefore, in how we present the Gospel to them. In no way do we want them to think that what we are offering is for sale.

We sin because we are weak humans. We have very little strength and will power. We may know what is right but we don't do it, at least we don't do it perfectly. Everyone we know is this way. They often talk good, but their actions don't match their words. But how can we be forgiven?

We must first recognize our lost state. And that no matter how righteousness we think we are or try to be, we always stand condemned before God because of who we are. I heard one TV personality express it like this: "We are sinners by nature, by choice, and by practice." I like to say that sin is what we do. Just like a lemon tree produces lemons or a grapevine produces grapes, sinners produce sin.

Once we recognize our sinful state, next we need to turn to God for forgiveness. This is the only way God has provided for us to remedy our situation. *"Then if my people who are called by my name will humbled themselves and pray and seek my face and turn from their wicked ways, I will hear from heaven and will forgive their sins and heal their land'"* (2 Chronicles 7:14). *"But the Lord our God is merciful and forgiving, even though we have rebelled [sinned] against him'"* (Daniel 9:9).

But let's put the concept of forgiveness in its proper prospective. God's love for us compels Him to forgive us. His love is everlasting; it continues forever:

"He prayed, 'O LORD, God of Israel, there is no God like you in all of heaven or earth. You keep your promises and show unfailing love to all who obey you and are eager to do your will" (1 Kings 8:23).

"*Give thanks to him who parted the Red Sea. His faithful love endures forever. He led Israel safely through, His faithful love endures forever. . . . Give thanks to him who led his people through the wilderness. His faithful love endures forever*" (Psalm 136:13–16).

"*Understand, therefore, that the* LORD *your God is indeed God. He is the faithful*

God who keeps his covenant for a thousand generations and constantly loves those who love him and obey his commands" (Deuteronomy 7:9).

But what about those who refuse to accept God's forgiveness? All such people remain under condemnation. If they remain in this state, they will be thrown into hell when Jesus returns: *"Therefore I will judge you, O house of Israel, every one according to his ways, saith the LORD GOD. Repent, and turn yourselves from all your transgressions; so iniquity shall not be your ruin. Cast away from you all your transgressions, whereby ye have transgressed; and make you a new heart and a new spirit: for why will ye die, O . . . Israel? For I have no pleasure in the death of him that dieth, saith the LORD GOD: wherefore turn yourselves, and live ye"* (Ezekiel 18:30–32, KJV).

Accepting God's forgiveness is an act of faith. We do not deserve God's forgiveness. Not even the best of us deserve it. But that's just the point. This is what makes this study on forgiveness so delightful. It takes us out of the realm of human understanding into the realm of revelation—the realm of the heavenly. In this, God is giving us something that comes from His unfathomable mind, not ours. He delights in doing things like this and will continue to do so forever.

God says of Himself in Isaiah 41: *"When the poor and needy search for water and there is none, and their tongues are parched from thirst, then I, the LORD, will answer them. I, the God of Israel, will never forsake them."*

The poor and needy are the lost of the world. The water they search for is God's mercy and forgiveness. God shows them love by providing just what they need.

He continues: *"I will open up rivers for them on high plateaus. I will give them fountains of water in the valleys. In the deserts, they will find pools of water. Rivers fed by springs will flow across the dry, parched ground."*

These references to water are types for the preaching of the Gospel and the indwelling Spirit of God. But none of this would be possible if our sins are not forgiven.

I don't think I can make this too clear. It was our sins that put Jesus on that cross. We are the ones who sinned. We are the ones who did wrong. Jesus didn't do anything wrong. It's like someone stepping in and taking a beating that was meant for us. And He did this of His own free will.

This was all pure love; nothing in the universe can be compared to it. It is greater than anything we can know and deeper than the deepest ocean. But the incredible thing is God deposits this love in those who trust in Him. This enables us to forgive people, whom we otherwise would not. Also, it enables us to love people who are otherwise unlovable.

Psalm 130:5–8 says, *"I am counting on the LORD; yes, I am counting on him. I have put my hope in his word. I long for the Lord more than sentries long for the dawn, yes, more than sentries long for the dawn.*

"O Israel, hope in the L<small>ORD</small>*; for with the* L<small>ORD</small> *there is unfailing love and an overflowing supply of salvation. He himself will free Israel from every kind of sin."*
Oh that we may understand!

4

SOME WORDS OF JESUS TO HIS SAINTS

In this chapter, I want to give you some specific facts about Jesus. And as you read this chapter, I hope that you will be encouraged to continue working for Jesus until the day He calls us home. This will count us among the saints beginning with righteous Abel, all the way up to the present.

Jesus told us in John 8:25–26, *"I am the one I have always claimed to be."* Who did He claim to be? He claimed to be the Son of God. To the Jews, that was a powerful statement, but if the Jews understood it, how much more true it should be for us today.

He continued, *"I have much to say about you and much to condemn, but I won't. For I say only what I have heard from the one who sent me, and he is true."* This is a reference to the mission given to Him by the Father. The Father sent Him on a rescue mission, one of rescuing lost souls. Many people get this confused. They think He came to condemn us. Have you ever heard preaching like this? Yes, we are condemned if we choose to stay in our sins, but that is our choice, not His.

That is the reason preaching is important. Our job is to warn sinners to stay away from hell. We tell them to turn to Jesus. We tell them to repent of their sins. We tell them that Jesus loves them. We tell them that Jesus wants them to be saved and go to heaven. And we tell them about the joys of heaven.

Verse 27 says that they still didn't understand what He was talking about. How shocking!

So Jesus told them in verses 28–29, *"When you have lifted up the Son of Man on the cross, then you will realize that I am he, and that I do nothing on my own, but speak what the Father taught me. And the one who sent me is with me—he has not deserted me. For I always do those things that are pleasing to him."*

The words, "lifted up the Son of Man" were directed specifically to the Jews, but in a more spiritual way to God's saints. We must remember that these words were spoken over two thousand years ago. Over this time, millions have heard these words and wondered what they mean. I will tell you: it was the sins of the saints that lifted Jesus up on that pole, for before the saints were saved, they were sinners.

As Jesus was walking along, He saw a man who had been blind from birth. Jesus made mention that the man had been born blind so that the glory of God would be revealed. By this, Jesus meant that just as people are blind in the physical sense, they are also blind spiritually. Namely, they can't see the light of God that shines in the face of the One God sent to save them. (John 9:1–3).

Jesus added in verses 4–5, *"All of us must quickly carry out the tasks assigned us by the one who sent me, because there is little time left before the night falls and all the work comes to an end. But while I am still here in the world, I am the light of the world."*

"All of us must quickly carry out the tasks assigned us"—in addition to being saved, God has given each of His saints individual tasks. Some of us are teachers, some of us are servers, and some of us are assigned to give words of encouragement. And some of us are assigned to give aide to others. But whatever our assignments are, they are part of a greater whole; that is, they serve to advance God's kingdom.

"There is little time left before night falls"—we don't know how long God will let us live. But whatever the length of time, we must do the very best we can. Anything less is a sin. Anything less, counts us like the servant who buried his master's money in the ground (Matthew 25:18). Yes, he gave it back, but that is not why God gave it to him. He was supposed to invest it in something that would bring God glory. This is what we all must do. Working for God to the best of our abilities gives God glory. And working to the best of our abilities proves that our faith is genuine.

Verse 8 adds: *"His neighbors and others who knew him as a blind beggar asked each other, 'Is this the same man—that beggar?' Some said he was, others said, 'No, but he surely looks like him!'"*

Did you catch that? God's saints are no longer recognized by the world. Yes, they see us, but they don't know us anymore. On the outside, we may look like the same person, but we are not. We talk different, we walk different, we act different, we think different, and we *are* different. This gives confusion to the people who know us. They think we are crazy or that something is seriously wrong. But it is not. We are just "new creatures in Christ."

Those who follow Jesus are walking in the light. Their eyes have been opened and they can see that the way they once lived is wrong. The lies they told are wrong. The sinful thoughts they once thought are wrong. The lust they once indulged in is wrong. The hate they held for others is wrong. The unforgiveness they held against others is wrong. But now they don't want to live this way anymore.

It is as if Jesus is saying to them, "You know the God who brought light to the world at the beginning of time? Well, that was Me. Just as I gave light to the world then, I give you light now. And with this light, you won't stumble in the darkness. My light will open your blind eyes. My light will brighten your day. My light will shine on your path. My light will expose all the wrong things that you once thought were right.

"The people around you are walking in darkness. They think they can see, but they can't. This is proven by the evil you see around you. Sin is everywhere. There's drug abuse. There are perversions of all kinds. Wars abound. People steal, lie, cheat, and murder. And you ask why they do this. Because they can't see. Thus, only when they walk in My light will they see well enough to walk in the right path."

Then Jesus healed the man. And when the people asked how he was healed, the man answered, *"The man they call Jesus made mud and smoothed it over my eyes and told me, 'Go to the pool of Siloam and wash off that mud.' I went and washed, and now I can see!"* (John 9:11).

All people living in sin have "mud on their eyes." They have been blinded by Satan. Their eyes are as if they are filled with the silt of their own deceitful ways and the mud of Satan's folly. They also stumble through the day as if it were night. But when the mud is washed off, everything changes.

When the Pharisees said that Jesus was a sinner and claimed that they didn't know anything about Him, the man made this reply: *"Why that's strange! He healed my eyes, and yet you don't know anything about him! Well, God doesn't listen to sinners, but he is ready to hear those who worship him and do his will. Never since the world began has anyone been able to open the eyes of someone born blind. If this man were not from God, he couldn't do it"* (John 9:30–33).

But Jesus was from God. God had sent Him into the world for moments just like this. In other words, He was sent to be a witness to these blind Pharisees. And not only to them but also to all who would set themselves up in opposition to His kingdom. But for those of us who submit to Him, His kingdom is an everlasting kingdom, bringing peace and joy to its subjects, and in the end, a home in heaven.

Along this line, Jesus said in Matthew 9:15: *"Should the wedding guest mourn while celebrating with the groom? Someday he will be taken away from them, and then they will fast."* This is a comparison of how people who walk with Christ act, as opposed to those who don't know Him. With Christ, there is constant celebration. The atmosphere is festive, as if there is a wedding feast taking place. This is not to say that things always go our way. But it does mean that even if things do go wrong, it will all be sorted out in the end.

The phrase "someday he will be taken away" is a figure of speech. It speaks of those who never knew Christ. They are in a state of mourning because they have no hope for heaven. All they have is the here and now, and they desperately fight to keep it. But the more they fight, the more it slips away. Then they look around and see gray hair and wrinkled faces, and they can't stop this either. No wonder they mourn!

Jesus said in verses 16–17: *"And who would patch an old garment with unshrunk cloth? For the patch shrinks and pulls away from the old cloth, leaving an even bigger hole than before. And no one puts new wine into old wineskins. The old skins would burst from the pressure, spilling the wine and ruining the skins. New wine must be stored in new wineskins. That way both the wine and the wineskins are preserved."*

Many apply these words to the Old Testament system of law, as opposed to the New Testament system of grace. And this is so. But it, too, is a type of our salvation. Before we are saved, we are like an old garment and an old wineskin. Trying to get us to live right is an impossibility. We need the infusion of the Holy Spirit that only Christ can give us. Then we are new persons. Now we can live right.

Jesus said to His saint Ezekiel (Ezekiel 33:2–3), *"Son of man, give your people this message. When I bring an army against a country, the people of that land choose a watchman. When the watchman sees the enemy coming, he blows the alarm to warn the people.'"*

Today, the saints of God are His watchmen. We see the terrible effects of sin around us. We see people blaspheming the name of God. And we see people acting any way they please. We warn them, then, that Christ will return and judge the world for its evil. And we warn them that those who refuse to repent will suffer the consequences.

Verses 4–5 say: *"Then if those who hear the alarm refuse to take action— well, it is their own fault if they die. They heard the warning but wouldn't listen, so the responsibility is theirs. If they had listened to the warnings they could have saved their lives."*

But the people of Ezekiel's day did not listen to God's saint. They kept right on sinning as if he was not even talking to them. Then the enemy came and carried them away to a strange land. But even in this land, Ezekiel's words were not heeded. Like people do today, they blamed God for their troubles. Like people do today, they said that God is not fair. And like people do today, they refused to take any responsibility for their sins. Today, many people don't believe that they do sin.

But among those rebellious people, there was a small group who did repent. Jesus said of them (Ezekiel 34:11–13): *"For this is what the Sovereign* LORD *says: I myself will search and find my sheep (I myself will search and find my saints). I will be like a shepherd looking for his scattered flock."* This is a picture of what He was later to say to us in John 10, and a picture of what He had already said in Psalm 23.

He continued: *"I will find my sheep and rescue them from all the places to which they were scattered on that dark and cloudy day. I will bring them back home to their own land of Israel from among the people and nations. . . ."*

Like sheep, we have all been scattered to distant levels of sin. Some of us sin more than others though. And some of us sin differently than others. But it makes no difference to God. Sin is like a long chain. If you break one of its links, you break the chain. We must remember that there are ten commandments. Just to list a few: Do not worship other gods, do not make idols, do not steal, do not kill, to not commit adultery, do not bear false witness, etc. But like the chain, if you break one commandment, you break them all.

But Jesus came to provide payment for sins no matter how bad they are. As testimony to this, He told us in Matthew 28 that He will be with us always and in all circumstances. And that He will do this even until the end of the world. He told us elsewhere that He will never leave us or forsake us.

Jesus came all the way from heaven and was born as a littler baby in a stable. He was obedient to His parents until He was thirty years old. Then He started His ministry. And the first thing He said to the people was to repent because the kingdom of heaven was at hand. This is a reference to God filling His saints with His Spirit and placing them in His church.

Our purpose in life, then, is to believe in Jesus so that He can place us in His church, and then to tell others to do the same. Solomon said it this way in Ecclesiastes 12:13: *"Here is my final conclusion: Fear God and obey his commands, for this is the duty of every person. God will judge us for everything we do, including every secret thing, whether good or bad."*

Now this same Jesus is coming back for His saints. I don't know when, because I don't set dates. But He is coming back! And when He does, we will look up and see Him as He descends, bringing with Him those who have gone before us, too. We will see Abraham, Isaac, Jacob, Job, Moses, and all the prophets of old. We will also see John the Baptist, Peter, Andrew, Levi, and Thomas. And then there are all the unnamed saints who have died since the Bible was written. We will see them too.

What a glorious day that will be!

I will close this chapter with the words of the song "Sanctify Me" by Rexband:

> Sanctify me Oh God
> Cleanse my body, mind and soul
> Purify me and make me whole.
> Help me to put off my old self
> Corrupted by all its deceitful desires

Create me anew in your likeness O Lord
Make me righteous and holy.
Let me not confirm any longer
To the pattern set by the ways of the world
... [Let me] offer myself as a living sacrifice
That is holy and pleasing.
Strengthen me with power through your Spirit
Transform me Christ in the full of ... [your] love
That I may perceive the length the breath the depth
And the height of ... [your great] love, Lord.[1]

---

1 "Sanctify Me song—Rexband," pp. 1–4, http://www.turnbacktogod.com/sanctify-me-song-rexband/; Internet; accessed 9 December 2010.

5

CHRISTIAN BAPTISM AND THE TRUMPETS

Just before He ascended to heaven, Jesus told His disciples, *"I have been given complete authority in heaven and on earth. Therefore, go and make disciples of all nations, baptizing them in the name of the Father and the Son and the Holy Spirit. Teach these new disciples to obey all the commands I have given you. And be sure of this: I am with you always, even to the end of the age"* (Matthew 28:18–20).

It is recorded this way in Mark 16:15–16: *"And then he told them, 'Go into . . . the world and preach the Good News to everyone, everywhere. Anyone who believes and is baptized will be saved. But anyone who refuses to believe will be condemned.'"* Verses 19–20 tell us, *"When the Lord Jesus had finished talking . . . he was taken into heaven and sat down in the place of honor at God's right hand. And the disciples went everywhere and preached, and the Lord worked with them, confirming what they said by many miraculous signs."*

As a child, I was baptized by my father when I was seven years old. I remember my father being very gentle with me. I was his son and he wanted everything to be right. He helped me to dress, and carefully led me into the water. I didn't understand what it meant, but I knew it was important. My father dipped me under the water, and as I came up, I felt good because I knew I was doing God's will. I will always remember this event as one of the highlights of my life.

Baptism is a beautiful ceremony. It is filled with pageantry and solemnity. Those who undergo this ritual submit themselves to a ritual that is steeped in tradition. From John the Baptist and Jesus to the Catholic Church, the Protestant Church, and all churches after, people have been baptized, and will continue to be baptized.

Much has already been written about the history of baptism, so I will forgo a discussion on this subject and concentrate on its meaning to the church. Let's look at Jesus' first miracle. John 2:1–10 records:

> *The next day Jesus' mother was a guest at a wedding celebration in the village of Cana in Galilee. Jesus and his disciples were also invited to the celebration. The wine supply ran out during the festivities, so Jesus mother spoke to him about the problem. "They have no more wine," she told him.*
>
> *"How does that concern me?" Jesus asked. "My time has not yet come." But his mother told the servants, "Do whatever he tells you."*
>
> *Six stone waterpots were standing there; they were used for Jewish ceremonial purposes and held twenty to thirty gallons each. Jesus told the servants, "Fill the jars with water." When the jars had been filled to the brim, he said, "Dip some out and take it to the master of ceremonies." So they followed his instructions.*
>
> *When the master of ceremonies tasted the water that was now wine, not knowing where it had come from (though, of course, the servants knew), he called the bridegroom over. "Usually a host serves the best wine first," he said. "Then, when everyone is full and doesn't care, he brings out the less expensive wines. But you have kept the best until now!"*

This proves that the Jews were already familiar with baptism. They did not use that specific name, of course, but the intent was the same. The waterpots held water used by the Jews to wash themselves before important religious rituals. The implication was that washing with water pictured the type of spiritual cleansing Christ would provide for the people when He came. Now the Jews may not have understood this, but Jesus certainly did. It was He who had told Moses to instruct the Jews on such types.

By Jesus changing the water into wine, it pictured us being changed into the image of Christ when we are saved. Wine pictures the blood of Christ, which makes our change possible. Water, then, pictures the Gospel by which we receive knowledge of salvation. Do you see the point?

Another reference is seen in John 13:3–6: *"Jesus knew that the Father had given him authority over everything and that he had come from God and would return to God. So he got up from the table, took off his robe, wrapped a towel around his waist, and poured water into a basin. Then he began to wash the disciples' feet and to wipe them with the towel he had around him."*

Peter did not want to submit to this ritual, but Jesus said that if he did not, he would not belong to Him; that is, he would not be clean.

This is what Jesus meant when He said to John, *"It must be done, because we must do everything that is right."* It is recorded in the King James translation, *"Suffer it to be so now: for thus it becometh us to fulfill all righteousness"* (Matthew 3:15). That is to say, "I am doing what is right by giving the people a picture of me, their long-awaited Savior. By the shedding of My blood, I will provide cleansing for not only the Jews, but for the entire world. This is what the law and the prophets are all about.

We don't realize how perfectly Jesus' life typed Old Testament law. In fact, His life so pictured the intent of the law that He said that not one little portion of the law would pass away until He had accomplished all the law pointed to. This means that the law will always be part of the Bible, even though its administration over us is made void by what Jesus did.

For example, there was the ceremony for cleansing people with bodily discharges. In this ceremony, Moses told the people that if they touched a person with a discharge, or something that had been in contact with him, they were to wash their clothing and bathe their bodies in water. But the people would be defiled until evening. After this, they would once again be allowed to have contact with other people.[1]

After a person with a discharge was healed, he was supposed to wait a period of seven days. During the seven days, he would wash his clothes and bathe himself in fresh spring water. Then the priest would declare the man ceremonially clean. On the eighth day, the priest would complete the procedure by making an offering of two birds to the Lord on the man's behalf (Leviticus 15:1–15)

Another example can be seen in the duties of Aaron, the high priest, on the Day of Atonement. As Aaron entered the sanctuary area, he would bring a young bull as a sin offering and a ram for a whole burnt offering. He would then wash his entire body and put on his linen tunic and the undergarments worn next to his body. After this, he would tie the linen sash around his waist and put the linen turban on his head. Now he was ready for his priestly duties (Leviticus 16:3–6)[2]

Paul said this about the Old Testament law of circumcision: *"When you came to Christ, you were 'circumcised,' but not by a physical procedure. It was a spiritual procedure—the cutting away of your sinful nature. For you were buried with Christ when you were baptized. And with him you were raised to a new life because you trusted the mighty power of God, who raised Christ from the dead"* (Colossians 3:11–12).

Paul made reference to this in Philippians 3:7–9 when he told us, *"I once thought all these things were so very important, but now I consider them worthless because of what Christ has done. Yes, everything else is worthless when compared with the priceless gain of knowing Christ Jesus my Lord. I have discarded everything else, counting it all as garbage, so that I may have Christ and become one with him.*

"I no longer count on my own goodness or my ability to obey God's law, but I trust Christ to save me. For God's way of making us right with himself depends on faith."

Psalm 51:7–9 records: *"Purify me from my sins, and I will be clean; wash me, and I will be whiter than snow. Oh, give me back my joy again; you have broken me—now let me rejoice. Don't keep looking at my sins. Remove the stain of my guilt."* Hebrews 10:21–22 reads: *"And since we have a great High Priest who rules over God's people, let us go right into the presence of God, with true hearts fully trusting him. [Truly] . . . our evil consciences have been sprinkled with Christ's blood to make us clean, and our bodies have been washed with pure water."*

But let's get back to baptism and Jesus. We said earlier that baptism was commanded by Jesus. And if Jesus commanded it, we should do it with joy. I know this is taking place because I see the peace and happiness that is displayed on the faces of those who submit to it. Their faces light up because they know that Jesus is pleased with them.

Titus 2:11–15 tells us, *"For the grace of God has been revealed, bringing salvation to all people. And we are instructed to turn from godless living and sinful pleasures. We should live in this evil world with self-control, right conduct, and devotion to God, while we look forward to that wonderful event when the glory of our great God and Savior, Jesus Christ, will be revealed. He gave his life to free us from every kind of sin, to cleanse us, and to make us his very own people, totally committed to doing what is right. You must teach these things and encourage your people to do them, correcting them when necessary. You have the authority to do this, so don't let anyone ignore you or disregard what you say."*

Let's say it this way. God sent Jesus into the world to cleanse us from our sins. He did this by dying on the cross. Then He was placed in a grave for three days, but on the third day, he was raised to life. This is what baptism pictures. We participate in this process by being baptized. Then we preach the Gospel to others.

But if we preach this Gospel the way God wants us to, we will be severely attacked by Satan and his demons. This attack is pictured most vividly in the seven trumpets of Revelation 8, 9, 11. We know these trumpets picture Satan's attack upon the preaching of the Gospel because this is the church's primary mission, and Satan has bound himself to stop it.

The trumpets themselves are representative of what happened at Mt. Sinai. As Jesus descended upon the mountain, the blast of a trumpet (shofar) was heard. Exodus 19:16–19 records: *"On the morning of the third day, there was a powerful thunder and lightning storm, and a dense cloud came down upon the mountain. There was a long, loud blast from a ram's horn, and all the people trembled. . . . As the horn blast grew louder and louder, Moses spoke and God thundered his reply for all to hear."*

There are seven trumpets in all, but the first six are symbolic and will not be heard. They are pictures of things that have been, are now, and are to come. But they are sounding now as I write this chapter. The seventh of these trumpets will be heard. It announces the coming of our Lord Jesus.

The first trumpet pictures Satan's attack upon the Gospel and those who believe in it. Sometimes this attack is direct; at other times, it comes under pretense. By pretense I mean that he pretends to be genuine, but his real intent is to deceive. This is pictured as one-third of the earth being set on fire and one-third of the green trees and the green grass burned. Green trees and green grass is a picture God's people. The one-third is symbolic of the number of people Satan will cause to stumble or fall.

The second trumpet pictures an attack upon the people who preach the Gospel. This is pictured as one-third of the sea turning to blood, and one-third of the ships of the sea being destroyed. The sea is the people who hear the Gospel, and the destroyed ships are the ministers who preach the Gospel.

The third trumpet pictures people rejecting God's Gospel. They also reject the Holy Spirit who helps them to believe. This is pictured as one-third of the rivers and spring water turning bitter. We must understand that the Gospel is sweet to those who believe. But to those who do not believe, it is bitter. The same is true of the Holy Spirit.

The fourth trumpet types Satan's attack on the church. This is pictured as one-third of the sun and one-third of the moon becoming dark. In other words, Satan's attack is so great that the smoke from its destruction blocks out the light of God's Gospel. This leaves people in darkness.

The fifth trumpet pictures Satan's setting loose his demons upon the earth. They attack the people of God with all their might. They are pictured as a horde of swarming locus. But although they attack us, they can't take our salvation.

Under the sixth trumpet, Satan's demons attack the unsaved of the world. The number of demons involved is 200 million. But the people refuse to repent. At this point God says He's had enough and will wait no longer.

The seventh trumpet, then, announces the return of Christ.

God bless you!

---

1 "Leviticus 15—Passage Lookup—New International Version . . .," pp. 1–3, http://www.biblegateway.com/passage/?search=Leviticus+15&version=NIV; Internet; accessed 8 January 2010.

2 "Leviticus 16—Passage Lookup—King James Version—BibleGateway.com," pp. 1–4, http://www.biblegateway.com/passage/?search=Leviticus+16&version=KJV; Internet; accessed 8 January 2009.

6

WHY THE CROSS?

In this chapter, we will solve a mystery that has perplexed Bible scholars for millennia. Specifically, why did God allow His Son Jesus to die on a Roman cross? The martyr, Steven, was stoned to death and John the Baptist was beheaded. James, the brother of John the Apostle, was killed with a sword. So why was Jesus killed on a cross?

It is my belief that God purposely chose the cross for Jesus. And that this choice was made in eternity, even before man was made. This is the way God is. He plans things in advance according to how He intends for them to work out. As humans, we don't understand this, nor can we duplicate it ourselves. But God is under no such limitations.

The Scripture reference for this is Ephesians 1:2–4: *"How we praise God, the Father of our Lord Jesus Christ, who has blessed us with every spiritual blessing in the heavenly realms because we belong to Christ. Long ago, even before he made the word, God loved us and chose us in Christ to be holy and without fault in his eyes."*

1 Peter 1:18–20 reads: *"For you know that God paid a ransom to save you from the empty life you inherited from your ancestors. And the ransom he paid was not mere gold or silver. He paid for you with the precious lifeblood of Christ, the sinless, spotless Lamb of God. God choose him for this purpose long before the world began. . . ."*

Think about it this way: God had planned all along, that if man sinned by eating of the forbidden tree, He would use the tree as the instrument of man's death. Why should it seem strange then, that God would use the same tree as the means of Christ's death, Christ being man's stand-in?

Let's see how this unfolded. We read in Genesis 2:15–17, *"The LORD God placed the man in the Garden of Eden to tend and care for it. But the LORD God gave him this warning: 'You may freely eat any fruit in the garden except fruit from the tree* of the knowledge of good and evil. If you eat of its fruit, you will surely die.'" This same decree is restated in Ezekiel 18:3–4: *"As surely as I live, says the Sovereign LORD, you will not say this proverb anymore in Israel. For all people are mind to judge—both parents and children alike. And this is my rule: The person who sins will be the one who dies."*

The New Testament gives us this same warning: *"And just as it is destined that each person dies only once and after that comes judgment, so also Christ died only once as a sacrifice to take away the sins of many people. He will come again but not to deal with our sins again. This time he will bring salvation to all those who are eagerly waiting for him"* (Hebrews 9:27–28).

That Adam's death was mandatory is borne out by what we read in Isaiah 40:6–8:

> *"A voice said, 'Shout!'*
> *"I asked, 'What should I shout?'*
> *"'Shout that people are like the grass that dies away. Their beauty fades as quickly as the beauty of flowers in a field. The grass withers, and the flowers fade beneath the breath of the LORD. And so it is with people. The grass withers, and the flowers fade, but the word of our God stands forever.'"*

Psalm 92:5–7 states: *"O LORD, what great miracles you do! And how deep are your thoughts. Only an ignorant person would not know this! Only a fool would not understand it. Although the wicked flourish . . . and evildoers blossom with success, there is only destruction ahead of them."*

But what if God had decided on another future for man? How would things have turned out then? But we don't have to speculate about this because the Bible does not. The Bible only reveals one plan for the salvation of man, and that plan is centered on Jesus.

The following Scriptures prove this point:

1. *"Don't you realize that I could ask the Father for thousands of angels to protect us, and he would send them instantly? But if I did, how would the Scriptures be fulfilled that describe what must happen now?"* (Matthew 26:53–54).
2. *"He was handed over to die because of our sins, and he was raised from the dead to make us right with God"* (Romans 4:25).
3. *"For even Christ didn't please himself . . ."* (Romans 15:3).

Let's restate it like this: Adam was supposed to die on a tree. Thus, we see Jesus dying on a tree in his place. But not only did He die in Adam's place, He died in our place too. That's why we don't see ourselves or Adam on the cross.

We could say that Adam is most fortunate indeed. He found someone who would come to the earth and take the punishment for what he did. And not only for what he did, but for what all his children would do. This is why Jesus is referred to in the Scriptures as the Second Adam. *"Nevertheless death reigned from Adam to Moses, even over them that had not sinned after the similitude of Adam's transgression, who is the figure of him that was to come"* (Romans 5:14, KJV).

But Christians have a different cross to bear. F. M. Perry noted:

> So what were the listeners to the words of Jesus to understand by this statement, *Whoever does not carry his own cross and come after Me cannot be My disciple?*
>
> The statement implies that people have a "cross," an instrument of death, to bear, and that they could only successfully deal with it by "taking it up" and following Jesus to become His disciple. I doubt that anyone fully understood this statement of Jesus at the time for it was not understood that such an instrument of death as a "cross" was to be involved in the lives of anyone, including even Jesus Himself.
>
> . . . Later, after Jesus had ascended to heaven, the Apostles received guidance from the Holy Spirit to understand the full meaning of His death and the "cross" upon which He died. Although the statements concerning a person's own "cross" were veiled at the time Jesus made them, they became clear as the prophecies contained in the statements were fulfilled, that is, **when Jesus Himself was tortured and put to death upon the "cross," which rightfully belonged to His followers!**
>
> So what does the statement mean to followers of Jesus today? Was Jesus speaking to Christians today when He said, *Let him deny himself, and take up his cross daily, and follow Me?* Yes. . . .
>
> I must understand that the "cross" that He bore was not His own. IT WAS MINE! It was the horrible symbol of the future that Satan had in mind for ME . . .[1]

F. M. Perry is saying we must picture ourselves being marched up Calvary's hill to be crucified for our own sins. How God would have worked out the details, we do not know. That is, we don't know when, where, or how He would have brought our crucifixion about. But when we arrive at the spot of execution, we see that Jesus has already taken our place! WHAT A WONDERFUL REVELATION!

We must all acknowledge this; otherwise, there is no salvation!

Verses 1, 2, 3, and 6 of the old Negro spiritual, "Surely He Died on Calvary," say it best:

> Refrain:
> *Calvary, Calvary*
> *Calvary, Calvary*
> *Calvary, Calvary*
> *Surely he died on Calvary.*
>
> Every time I think about Jesus
> Every time I think about Jesus
> Every time I think about Jesus
> Surely he died on Calvary.
>
> Don't you hear the hammer ringing?
> Don't you hear the hammer ringing?
> Don't you hear the hammer ringing?
> Surely he died on Calvary.
>
> Don't you hear him calling his Father?
> Don't you hear him calling his Father?
> Don't you hear him calling his Father?
> Surely he died on Calvary.
>
> Sinners, do you love my Jesus?
> Sinner, do you love my Jesus?
> Sinner, do you love my Jesus?
> Surely he died on Calvary.[2]

But most people don't want to hear these types of songs today. Church music today is born out of the cultural revolution of the 1960s. It emphasized self-worth, the potential of man, man's future, our temporal needs, relationships, etc. And even when it does mention Christ, He is generally presented as a benevolent benefactor without any mention of His atoning death.

This is most unfortunate because it robs us of the loving relationship we could have with the person who gave His all for us. He did not have to do this, you know. But He did. He could have stayed in heaven with the Father. He could have stayed in heaven with the holy angels, receiving their praise and worship, unceasingly. This would have prevented all the pain He suffered, and the grief and humiliation that goes along with it. But then, we would have no salvation.

This was not the case in the old days. I can remember people singing songs such as "All Hail the Power," "Come Thou Almighty King," "A Mighty

Fortress Is our God," and "At the Cross." But these songs are no longer popular because they don't appeal to most people.

But Jesus is our sin-bearer. He bore our sins on a lonely tree, a tree that we should have hung on. This makes Him the ultimate hero, and the ultimate champion of the human race. The first Adam was no hero and no champion. He left us a legacy of shame and defeat, and a destroyed world. But thank God, Jesus set things straight.

But still, God loves us in spite of ourselves. This love is eternal and without fault. It is overwhelming and up to the task. Psalm 26:1–3 states: *"Declare me innocent, O LORD, for I have acted with integrity; I have trusted in the LORD without wavering. Put me on trial, LORD, and cross-examine me. Test my motives and affections. [Truly] . . . I am constantly aware of your unfailing love, and I have lived according to your truth."*

At first, this seems to be speaking of David and his love for God. And it is, but its spiritual intent in unmistakable. This speaks of Jesus and His relationship with the Father. Who else could say that he is innocent of sin, full of integrity, full of trust in God, and has lived according to God's truth?

The point is just as Jesus places His trust in God, God's love for us compelled Him to send Jesus into the world to demonstrate that love!

Still, though, we must choose to trust in this love. Joshua said it this way: *"So honor the LORD and serve him wholeheartedly. Put away forever the idols your ancestors worshiped when they lived beyond the Euphrates River and in Egypt. Serve the LORD alone. But if you are unwilling to serve the LORD, then choose today whom you will serve. Would you prefer the gods your ancestors served beyond the Euphrates? Or will it be the gods of the Amorites in whose land you now live? But as for me and my family, we will serve the LORD"* (Joshua 24:14–15).

Deuteronomy 11:26–32 reads: *"Today I am giving you the choice between a blessing and a curse! You will be blessed if you obey the commands of the LORD your God that I am giving you today. You will receive a curse if you reject the commands of the LORD your God and turn from his way by worshiping foreign gods.*

"'When the LORD your God brings you into the land to possess it, you must pronounce a blessing from . . . Gerizim and a curse from Mount Ebal. . . . For you are about to cross the Jordan to occupy the land the LORD your God is giving you. When you are living in that land, you must be careful to obey all the laws and regulations I am giving you today.'"

The prophet Jeremiah was trusting in God's love when he lamented this: *"The Lord in his anger has cast a dark shadow over Jerusalem. The fairest of Israel's cities lies in the dust, thrown down from the heights of heaven. In his day of awesome fury, the Lord has shown no mercy even to his Temple.*

"Without mercy the Lord has destroyed every home in Israel. In his anger, he has broken down the fortress walls of Jerusalem. He has brought to dust the kingdom and its

rulers" (Lamentations 2:1–2).

The prophet is saying that the people of Jerusalem sinned, and they were destroyed. But God later restored them. This is a type of what the cross of Christ did for us, i.e., it restored us to God, making us His friends again.

How many people are listening though? For the sake of the human race, I hope that many are. This is a critical moment. It is a time when Satan seems to be intensifying his activities. Our bodies may not be in danger, but our souls are. Satan will capture them if we are not careful. Let us set our eyes back on the cross of Christ, and thank Him every day for what He has done for us.

As well, let us serve Jesus with all our hearts, souls, and minds. And as Paul said, run the race set before us until we reach the finish line. When we get there, we will see that Jesus was right there with us all along. He was right there with us when we needed Him the most. In fact, it was Jesus who inspired us to endure in the first place—a further testimony to His love for us.

Just think of it, God coming to earth, taking on a human body, and dying in the place of man. Yes, there were Scriptures in the Old Testament pointing to this event. But who believed them? Who would have thought it was possible? The prophet Isaiah captured this thought when he said, *"Who has believed our message? To whom will the* LORD *reveal his saving power?"* (Isaiah 53:1).

Then he went on to tell us (verses 2–3): *"My servant grew up in the* LORD*'s presence like a tender green shoot, sprouting from a root in dry and sterile ground. There was nothing beautiful or majestic about his appearance, nothing to attract us to him. He was despised and rejected—a man of sorrows, acquainted with the bitterest grief.*

"We turned our backs on him and looked the other way when he went by. He was despised, and we didn't care."

But thank God, some of us repented of this and now we care!

Isaiah concluded then (verse 11): *"When he sees all that is accomplished by his anguish, he will be satisfied. And because of what he has experienced, my righteous servant will make it possible for many to be counted righteous, for he will bear their sins."*

Our God actually did this. This is no myth. This was a real event, and we can put our trust in it. Jesus did grow up as a root in dry ground, that is, the society in which he lived rejected Him. He was not handsome and was no idol of adoration. He was despised by those who should have loved Him. But His death made many righteous. And because of this, He is now seated at "God's right hand" in heaven (Matthew 26:64).

We see Jesus' death foreshadowed by the incident of a bronze snake in the wilderness (Numbers 21:4–9). There, as God led the people around Edom to the Promised Land, they stopped at a selected spot to rest. Then the people started to complain and murmur against God and Moses. *"Why have you brought us out of Egypt to die here in the wilderness?"* they protested. *"There is nothing to eat here and nothing to drink. And we hate this wretched manna!"*

Because of this, God sent poisonous snakes among them. Many of them died from poisonous snake bites. Then the people cried to Moses, *"We have sinned by speaking against the* LORD *and against you. Pray that the* LORD *will take away the snakes."* Then, God said to Moses, *"Make a replica of a poisonous snake and attach it to the top of a pole. Those who are bitten will live if they simply look at it!"* After that, the Bible records: *"So Moses made a snake out of bronze and attached it to the top of a pole. Whenever those who were bitten looked at the bronze snake, they recovered!"*

This is a lesson for us today; our souls are in danger of destruction. But like the people in the wilderness, we must look up to Christ on the cross and live!

Hebrews 12:1–2 says it this way: *"Therefore, since we are surrounded by such a huge crowd of witnesses to the life of faith, let us strip off every weight that slows us down, especially the sin that so easily hinders our progress. And let us run with endurance the race that God has set before us. We do this by keeping our eyes on Jesus, on whom our faith depends from start to finish. . . ."*

Jesus constantly spoke of His death. *". . . Then a voice spoke from heaven saying, 'I have already brought it glory, and I will do it again.' When the crowd heard the voice, some thought it was thunder, while others declared an angel had spoken to him. Then Jesus told them, 'The voice was for your benefit, not mine. The time of judgment for the world has come, when the prince of this world will be cast out. And when I am lifted up on the cross, I will draw everyone to myself.' He said this to indicate how he was going to die,"* John 12:28–33 tells us.

We read in Mark 8:31–33: *"Then Jesus began to tell them that he, the Son of man, would suffer many terrible things and be rejected by the leaders, the leading priest, and the teachers of religious law. He would be killed, and three days later he would rise again. As he talked about this openly with his disciples, Peter took him aside and told him he shouldn't say things like that.*

"Jesus turned and looked at his disciples and then said to Peter very sternly, 'Get away from me, Satan! You are seeing things merely from a human point of view, not from God's."

The Bible tells us that the people came out of Egypt loaded with silver and gold—they "plundered" the Egyptians of their valuable items! But this silver and gold did not save them; those who refused to look to Christ still died!

What's more, God rained down all sorts of miracles on the people. He opened up the Red Sea, led them by a pillar of fire by night and a pillar of cloud by day, made water come out of a rock, turned bitter water sweet, and made their clothes last for forty years. In addition, He gave them quail and manna to eat, turned back the Jordan River, and made the walls of Jericho fall down. Nevertheless, these miracles didn't make them turn to God.

The Bible says:

> *After that generation died, another generation grew up who did not acknowledge the LORD or remember the mighty things he had done for Israel. Then the Israelites did what was evil in the LORD's sight and worshiped the images of Baal. They abandoned the LORD, the God of their ancestors, who had brought them out of Egypt. They chased after other gods, worshiping the gods of the people around them. And they angered the LORD. They abandoned the LORD to serve Baal and the images of Ashtoreth.*
>
> *This made the LORD burn with anger against Israel, so he handed them over to marauders who stole their possessions. He sold them to their enemies all around, and they were no longer able to resist them. Every time Israel went out to battle, the LORD fought against them, bringing them defeat, just as he promised. And the people were very distressed* (Judges 2:10–15).

Paul tells us this about Christ: *"Well then, what shall we say about these things? Just this: The Gentiles have been made right with God by faith, even though they were not seeking him. But the Jews, who tried so hard to get right with God by keeping the law, never succeeded. Why not? Because they were trying to get right with God by keeping the law and being good instead of by depending on faith. They stumbled over the great rock in their path. God warned them of this in the Scriptures when he said, 'I am placing a stone in Jerusalem that causes people to stumble, and a rock that makes them fall. But anyone who believes in him will not be disappointed'"* (Romans 9:30–33).

"Yes, he is very precious to you who believe," Peter tells us. *"But for those who reject him, 'The stone that was rejected by the builders has now become the cornerstone.' And the Scriptures also say, 'He is the stone that makes people stumble, the rock that will make them fall.' They stumble because they do not listen to God's word or obey it, and so they meet the fate that has been planned for them.*

"But you are not like that, for you are a chosen people. You are a kingdom of priests, God's holy nation, his very own possession. This is so you can show others the goodness of God, for he called you out of the darkness into his wonderful light" (1 Peter 2:7–9).

The Romans put Jesus to death at the behest of the Jews. That they did not know what they were doing, there is no doubt. But we know what we are doing today. We have the witness of the Scriptures and the preaching of the Gospel to instruct us. Therefore, if we reject what Jesus did for us, we are guilty of a far greater crime, one that is punishable by death. GOD, HELP US NOT TO DO THIS!

This is the true and honest Gospel of God!

---

1 "To Carry One's Own Cross," pp. 1–3, http://www.spiritofprayer.com/weavers/carrycross.html; Internet; accessed 16 January 2010.

2 "Surely He Died on Calvary," pp. 1–3, http://www.gospelsonglyrics.org/songs/surely_he_died_on_calvary.html; Internet; accessed January 2010.

PART 2
GOD AS THE CHRIST

7

JESUS THE CHRIST

The most significant person in the history of the world is Jesus Christ. To the Jews, He was the anointed One to come, the One who would free them from Roman rule and restore the lost kingdom of David. But to Christians, He is the One who will save us from our sins and fulfill all our hopes of heaven.

But most people are not looking for Christ in any capacity. You say His name and they turn away. Some get busy with meaningless tasks to distract our attention. Some become outright hostile. Others point out that other religions have their Christs too. "How you can claim that the Christ you preach is the right one?" they ask. Or "How do you know that He can save you?"

But listen to what David said about this in Psalm 2:1–5: *"Why do the nations rage? Why do the people waste their time with futile plans? The kings of the earth prepare for battle; the rulers plot together against the* Lord *and against his anointed one. 'Let us break their chains,' they cry, 'and free ourselves from this slavery.' But the one who rules in heaven laughs. The Lord scoffs at them. Then in anger he rebukes them. . . ."*

The nations are in a rage. And sadly, this rage is against the One who made them. They may not say this specifically, but it is true. The Bible declares that if we are angry with our brother, we are really angry against God (1 John 4:20). And this is the trouble with the world. People fight and kill each other, they tell lies on each other, they cheat each other, and they covet each other's property, all because they don't have a love relationship with Christ.

The plans of the people are futile because they don't include God in them. I am not talking about temporal plans. We can often bring these about.

I am talking about SPIRITUAL PLANS, that is, plans that test our love for God and our love for the people God created. Social scientists refer to these plans as social relations. This is why we see social unrest even among God's own people.

It is so sad that people feel this way about God. But as the Bible declares, God laughs at their feeble efforts!

In contrast to the plots of man, Jesus declares: *"For I, the LORD, love justice. I hate robbery and wrongdoing. I will faithfully reward my people for their suffering and make an everlasting covenant with them. Their descendants will be known and honored among the nations. Everyone will realize that they are a people the LORD has blessed"* (Isaiah 61:8–9).

I am amazed at how true this is. God allows us to go our own way, and how people take advantage of this. We wonder when these people will receive justice, especially if they mistreat us, or take advantage of us in some way. But God is not interested in dispensing justice on a temporal basis (for every little thing people do wrong now). If so, very few people would be left alive.

It's like this. We say that people will pay for their sins, meaning they will pay for them before they leave this world. But we don't see this taking place. We see the wicked prospering. Many of them go on to have great careers, or are otherwise successful in life. People flock to their support. They are proclaimed heroes. This is especially true when the offender does something we agree with. But God is not asleep. He sees what is taking place.

God will punish the wicked at the last day when He separates the "sheep from the goats" and the "good from the evil." This is spoken of all through the four Gospels, especially in Matthew 25. But until then, we must wait in hope, knowing that God knows what's best for us.

In verse 10, Isaiah says, *"I am overwhelmed with joy in the LORD my God! [Truly,] . . . he has dressed me with the clothing of salvation and draped me in a robe of righteousness. I am like a bridegroom in his wedding suit or a bride with her jewels."*

Isaiah didn't have an easy time preaching to evil people. But because of the promises of God, he looked forward to the joys to come. He compared himself to a glowing bride awaiting her wedding day. The bride may have apprehensions now, but she is sure that her bridegroom will come and her wedding will soon take place. This gives her hope and great pleasure. This is the state of the righteous as we await our wedding day.

Zachariah 9:9–10 tells us, *"Rejoice greatly, O people of Zion! Shout in triumph, O people of Jerusalem! Look, your king is coming to you. He is righteous and victorious, yet he is humble, riding on a donkey—even on a donkey's colt. I will remove the battle chariots from Israel and the warhorses from Jerusalem, and I will destroy all the weapons used in battle. Your king will bring peace to the nations. His realm will stretch from sea to sea and from the Euphrates River to the ends of the earth"*

Didn't Jesus ride into Jerusalem on a donkey? And when He did, the people tried to make Him a temporal king, one in the line of the kings they were familiar with. But He was not that kind of king. His kingdom is within us. He rules in our hearts by His Spirit, giving us new hearts and new lives. This is how the "weapons of battle" are destroyed; He removes hate and malice from our minds, giving us, instead, peace and joy.

Isaiah spoke of this peace as the wolf and the lamb living together. That is, by God's Spirit we don't have the desire to fight anymore. Now we see the advantage of living in peace with all those who will allow us. I am not saying everyone will allow it though, but for those who do, we will live in friendship.

Isaiah further states that the leopard and the goat will be at peace, lions and calves will be at peace, bears and cattle will be at peace, and little children will be able to play with snakes. Then he says that nothing will hurt us if we put our trust in God. That is, yes, storms will come, but they won't be able to take away the peace we have from knowing Jesus as our Savior (Isaiah 11).

Listen to this: *"In that day you will sing: 'Praise the LORD! He was angry with me, but now he comforts me. See, God has come to save me. I will trust in him and not be afraid. The LORD GOD is my strength and my song; he has become my salvation'"* (Isaiah 12:1–2).

Verses 3–6 state: *"With joy you will drink deeply from the fountain of salvation! In that wonderful day you will sing: 'Thank the LORD! Praise his name! Tell the world what he has done. Oh, how mighty he is! Sing to the LORD, for he has done wonderful things. Make known his praise around the world. Let all the people of Jerusalem shout his praise with joy! For great is the Holy One of Israel who lives among you.'"*

Praise is one of the things God's people are known for. We don't praise God in a vacuum, however. We know what we are praising God for. It is because of John 3:16—God loves us so much—that He sent Jesus to die in our place on a lonely tree. This is what Isaiah means when he says that we will *"drink deeply from the fountain of salvation."* This fountain is so deep that we don't have words to express it. We just break out in shouts of joy. Sometimes we don't say anything at all; we just express our praise in our hearts or by the things we do for Jesus.

But let me make this point. Praise is not limited to a song service. Song services are good, but the spiritual implications of praise are more far reaching. What about people who are not chosen for this duty? What about people who can't sing? They would be left out. And what about the people who arrive late and miss this part of the service?

True spiritual praise comes from deep in our hearts, from deep in our souls. Our souls are so full of joy that we burst open with gratitude. This gratitude can be expressed in a variety of ways. For example, the prophet Isaiah didn't do a lot of singing like David did. He just spoke the words Jesus gave him to say. John the Baptist expressed his praise the same way. In his case, he stood by the Jordan River and shouted to the people.

Isaiah spoke of John's preaching when he said:

"Comfort, comfort my people," says your God. "Speak tenderly to Jerusalem. Tell her that her sad days are gone and that her sins are pardoned. Yes, the LORD has punished her in full for her sins."

Listen! I hear the voice of someone shouting, "Make a highway for the LORD through the wilderness. Make a straight smooth road through the desert for our God. Fill the valleys and level the hills. Straighten out the curves and smooth off the rough spots. Then the glory of the LORD will be revealed, and all people will see it together. The LORD has spoken!" (Isaiah 40:1–5).

Messenger of good news, shout to Zion from the mountain-tops! Shout louder to Jerusalem—do not be afraid. Tell the towns of Judah, "Your God is coming!" Yes, the Sovereign LORD is coming in all his glorious power. He will rule with awesome strength. See, he brings his reward with him as he comes. He will feed his flock like a shepherd. He will carry the lambs in his arms, holding them close to his heart. He will gently lead the mother sheep with the young" (Isaiah 40:9–11).

Let me make this statement about good preaching. Good preaching is not centered on stories about the lives of people, etc. Good preaching is centered on the death, burial, and resurrection of Jesus. In John the Baptist's case, he was to speak to the people and tell them that because of Jesus, their sad days were over. We can say it this way; before Jesus came, they were trapped in sin with no way out. Sin had complete mastery over them and was about to send them to hell. But now that Jesus was about to make His ministry public, all of this was about to end.

Then John was to make a smooth road for Jesus. This is the same mission we have today. We tell people that Jesus has come to save them. Then when He begins to make changes in their lives, they will know it is Him and proudly proclaim, "Yes, Jesus did this for me, and He will do the same for you."

But most important of all, John was to say to the people, "Your God is coming!" Did you get this? Your God is on the way and will soon appear among you! This is the most important proclamation preachers can make: "The man I am preaching to you is God, Himself, and He has come to save you."

Psalm 46:1–3 says this about Jesus as God: *"God is our refuge and strength, always ready to help in times of trouble. So we will not fear, even if earthquakes* come and the mountains crumble into the sea. Let the oceans roar and foam. Let the mountains tremble as the waters surge!"

So yes, your God is coming, and He is the Christ!

The word *Christ* means the "anointed one." This is pictured by the anointing oil God told the people to prepare in Exodus 30:23–33:

> Collect choice spices—12½ pounds of pure myrrh, 6¼ pounds each of cinnamon and of sweet cane, 12½ pounds of cassia [scented bark], and one gallon of olive oil. Blend these ingredients into . . . holy anointing oil. Use this scented oil to anoint the Tabernacle, the Ark of the Covenant, the table and all its utensils, the . . . [lamp stand] and all its accessories, the incense altar, the altar of burnt offering with all its utensils, and the large washbasin with its pedestal.
>
> Sanctify them to make them entirely holy. After this, whatever touches them will become holy. Use this oil also to anoint Aaron and his sons, sanctifying them so they can minister before me as priests. And say to the people of Israel, *"This will always be my holy anointing oil. It must never be poured on the body of an ordinary person, and you must never make any of it for yourselves.*
>
> *"It is holy, and you must treat it as holy. Anyone who blends scented oil like it or puts any of it on someone who is not a priest will be cut off from the community."*

Each of the ingredients blended into this oil represent the sweet flavor of Christ as He presents Himself to God for His service. The oil, itself, pictures the work of God in preparing Christ for His work, i.e., God poured out His Spirit upon Him without limit (Isaiah 61:1). This is why a warning is given against using this oil for an unspecified purpose.

In early Christian times, sick people were anointed for healing to take place. But this is not to say that God asks us to heal people today. Yes, God can heal, and often does, but the healing we should seek as born-again believers is to have our sins washed away and our names written in the Lamb's Book of Life.

Peter says the same thing: "I see very clearly that God doesn't show partiality. In every nation he accepts those who fear him and do what is right. I'm sure you have heard about the Good News for the people of Israel—that there is peace with God through Jesus Christ, who is Lord of all. . . .

> *And no doubt you know that God anointed Jesus of Nazareth with the Holy Spirit and with power. Then Jesus went around doing good*

and healing all who were oppressed by the Devil, for God was with him. And we apostles are witnesses of all he did throughout Israel and in Jerusalem. They put him to death by crucifying him, but God raised him to life three days later. Then God allowed him to appear, not to the general public, but to us whom God had chosen beforehand to be his witnesses. We were those who ate and drank with him after he rose from the dead. And he ordered us to preach everywhere and to testify that Jesus is ordained of God to be the judge of all—the living and the dead. He is the one all the prophets testified about, saying that everyone who believes in him will have their sins forgiven through his name (Acts 10:34-43).

But some may ask, "What about the special anointing God places on many Christians?"

Just because our assignments may be different, no one is more anointed than another is. *"We are all one body, we have the same Spirit, and we have all been called to the same glorious future"* (Ephesians 4:4). This makes God's people equal in His eyes, with equal shares in the kingdom of heaven. That is, God does not prop up one person over another.

May God bless you for reading these words!

8

IS JESUS GOD?

In the Bible, we are plainly told that Jesus is God (John 1:1). Jesus says of Himself in Revelation 1:8, *"I am the Alpha and the Omega—the beginning and the end. I am the one who is, who always was, and who is still to come, the Almighty One."* In the book of Titus, Paul calls Jesus, *"God our Savior"* (Titus 3:4). However, many people still do not believe that He is the Most High God.

But He is. And I will prove this in this chapter. This will be done by looking into the nature and character of God—His makeup and general disposition. Also, I will look into the character and nature of the three persons who make up God.

But some will say, "Isn't Jesus God's Son?" Yes, He is, but being God's Son does not keep Him from being God. This is the only way His death on the cross would have had any meaning. The Bible plainly tells us that only the Creator God, Himself, is able to save His creation by dying for them:[1]

"As for God, his way is perfect. All the LORD*'s promises prove true. He is a shield for all who look to him for protection. For who is God except the* LORD*? Who but our God is a solid rock? God arms me with strength; he has made my way safe. He makes me as surefooted as a deer, leading me safely along the mountain heights. He prepares me for battle; he strengthens me to draw a bow of bronze. You have given me the shield of your salvation . . ."* (Psalm 18:30–35).

The belief that Jesus is God is what makes our religion meaningful. Through Jesus, our one God supplies all our needs, giving us all the strength and courage we need to follow Him to the best of our abilities and to find our way into the glories of heaven. In other words, in Jesus, we have everything we need to be saved.

Pagan religions are not like this. They have a god for the city, a god for the country, a god for the hills, etc. In addition, they have gods who bless families, gods who bless crops, and gods who bless wine and bread. See what confusion this produces? See what dismay it causes? Who would know which one to pray to?

Yes, our God is a Trinity: Father, Son, and Holy Spirit. But He is not divided into three separate parts, as some have imagined. What I am saying is, what Moses said about Him in Deuteronomy 6:4–5 is true: *"Hear, O Israel! The LORD is our God, the LORD alone. And you must love the LORD your God with all your heart, all your soul, and all your strength."*

The King James Version translates these verses: *"Hear, O Israel: The LORD our God is one LORD: And thou shalt love the LORD thy God with all thine heart, and with all thy soul, and with all thy might."* This places the Old Testament and the New Testament in agreement. We can express it like this: the Old Testament states that God is one, and the New Testament confirms it by telling us how God is one.

Frances J. Beckwith says it this way:

> The Christian doctrine of the Trinity is part of every major creed in the history of Christendom. It can be defined in the following way: In the nature of the one God there are three centers of consciousness, which we call persons, and these three are equal. Though the term "trinity" is not found in the Bible, the doctrine is nevertheless taught there. "Trinity" is merely the term employed by theologians and church historians in order to describe the phenomena of God they find in the Bible.
>
> Let us review our argument for the Trinity. First, we showed that the Bible teaches that there is only one God. Second, we found that the Bible tells us that there are three persons called God. Hence, the inescapable conclusion: the three persons are the One God. Theologians have called this the Trinity.[2]

This means that the distinct person of the Son exists within God as a co-equal with God's other two persons. In other words, in the human body of Jesus lives the Father, the Son, and the Holy Spirit, but only the Son speaks to us. By "speak," I mean that only the Son identifies Himself.

This is proven by the fact that when the One God appeared on earth, He called Himself Jesus (Matthew 1:20–21): *"As he considered this, he fell asleep, and an angel of the Lord appeared to him in a dream. 'Joseph, son of David,' the angel said, 'do not be afraid to go ahead with your marriage to Mary. For the child within her* has been conceived by the Holy Spirit. And she will have a son, and you are to name him Jesus, for he will save his people from their sins.'"

The same is seen all through the four Gospels, and in the writings of Paul too. Yes, the Father and the Holy Spirit are often mentioned, but any direct words spoken by God are always identified as coming from the distinct person of Jesus. The same in evidenced in the book of Revelation, and the other books of the New Testament. Even when God returns at the last day, He will still identify Himself as Jesus.

(I will have much to say about the Father and Holy Spirit later.)

Another way to say this is God has personal traits or characteristics that make God—God the Father, God the Holy Spirit, and God the Son. Each of these distinct traits is the full expression of God, making Him God, Himself! So when Jesus speaks to us, it is another way of saying God speaks to us.

Many people get confused when they see verses in the Bible that say that Jesus, the Son, is "begotten" by God (John 1:14, KJV), or verses that seem to imply that Jesus was "generated" by God (John 5:26). But they shouldn't be.

Yes, Jesus was begotten by God. But this is true only in the sense that from eternity, God declared to the world that Jesus would be called His Son. To *declare* means to "make clear" or "to state emphatically."[3] In other words, from eternity, God made it clear by stating emphatically to all who would listen that His second person, the self-expressions He speaks through, would have the name, Son of God:

"I will proclaim the decree of the LORD*: He said to me, 'You are my Son, today I have become your Father'"* (Psalm 2:7, NIV). It is rendered in the King James Version, *"I will declare the decree: the* LORD *hath said unto me, Thou art my Son; this day have I begotten thee."*

The same is true when it comes to Jesus' human birth. When Jesus was born as a human being, Joseph was not His Father, God was (Matthew 1:18–25). God did this through the power of the Holy Ghost. Jesus was the only one begotten this way. Thus He was the only begotten Son of God (John 1:14, 18).

In the same sense then, Jesus was generated by God!

As a member of the Godhead, Jesus was always with the Father. It is stated this way in verses 1–3 of 1 John1: *"The one who existed from the beginning is the one we have heard and seen. We saw him with our own eyes and touched him with our own hands. He is Jesus Christ, the Word of Life. This one who is life from God was shown to us, and we have seen him. And now we testify and announce to you that he is eternal life. He was with the Father, and then he was shown to us. We are telling you about what we ourselves have actually seen and heard, so that you may have fellowship with us. And our fellowship is with the father and with his Son, Jesus Christ."*

We are not talking about three different Gods. This is expressly forbidden by the Scriptures. What we are talking about are three distinct persons existing simultaneously, within God. When you get God (the One God), you get all three of His persons since God is one. You can't have one of God's persons without having the other two as well.[4] For example, when the Holy Spirit lives in us, the Father and the Son live in us too (John 14:15–26).

But we can tell God's persons apart by what is said about each in the Bible. That is, the Bible makes a clear distinction between each of the persons. For example, Galatians 1:1 states, *"This letter is from Paul, an apostle. I was not appointed by any group or by human authority. My call is from Jesus Christ himself and from God the Father, who raised Jesus from the dead."*

Ephesians 1:3 states, *"How we praise God, the Father of our Lord Jesus Christ, who has blessed us with every spiritual blessing in the heavenly realms because we belong to Christ. Long ago, even before he made the world, God loved us and chose us in Christ to be holy and without fault in his eyes."* Then Luke 2:26 reads, *"The Holy Spirit had revealed to him that he would not die until he had seen the Lord's Messiah."*

The Internet article, "Can You Explain the Trinity," states the following: "'Trinity' is a . . . word used to describe what is apparent about God in the Scriptures. The Bible clearly speaks of God the Father, God the Son (Jesus Christ), and God the Holy Spirit . . . and also clearly presents that there is only one God. . . . Thus the term: 'Tri' meaning three, and 'Unity' meaning one, Tri+Unity = Trinity. It is a way of acknowledging what the Bible reveals to us about God, that God is yet three 'Persons' who have the same essence of deity. . . . God the Son (Jesus) is fully, completely God. God the father is fully, completely God. And God the Holy Spirit is fully, completely God. Yet there is one God. . . ."[5]

J. H. Keathley says this about God:

> In most formularies the doctrine is stated by saying that God is . . . [One] in his essential being, but that in his being there are three Persons, yet so as not to form separate . . . individuals. . . . 'Persons' is, however, an imperfect expression of the truth . . . as the term denotes to us a separate rational and moral individual. *But in the being of God there are not three individuals, but three self-distinctions within the one divine essence* [italics . . .].
>
> Then again, personality in man implies independence of will, actions and feelings leading to behavior peculiar to the person. This cannot be thought of in connection with the Trinity. Each person is self-conscious and self-directing, yet never acting independently or in opposition. When we say

that God is a Unity we [actually] mean that, though God is
. . . a threefold center of life, his life is not split into three.
He is one in essence, in personality and in will. When we
say that God is a Trinity . . . we mean that there is a unity in
diversity, and that the diversity manifests itself in Persons, in
characteristics and in operations.[6]

The Jews were amazed when Jesus mentioned the other members of the Godhead. This was a new revelation to them. Jesus was bringing them into full awareness of the triune God, in all His splendor and glory. He was revealing to them details that would make it possible for them (and us, also) to have a personal relationship with not only the Son, but with the Father and Holy Spirit, as well (John 17:3).

God had given the Jews a glimpse of His triune nature through the writings of Moses, but they did not understand it. For instance, we are told in Genesis 1:26, *"Then God said, 'Let us make people in our image, to be like ourselves. . . .'"* In Genesis 11:7 (KJV) God said, *"Go to, let us go down, and confound their language, that they may not understand one another's speech."* Isaiah 6:8 (KJV) states: *"Also I heard the voice of the Lord, saying . . . [whom] shall I send, and who will go for us? Then said I, Here am I; send me."*

These examples should be a witness to Christians who think along the line that some cults do. Some of them insist on denying the clear meaning of these Scriptures. They say that the "us" mentioned is a reference to God and the angelic hosts. Or that God is using figurative language the way famous personalities do. But this is not the case, and never will be. The Bible is very clear on this. All we have to do is to accept it.

That God would come to the earth in the person of His son should be no surprise to us. Mention is made of this all through the Old Testament; maybe we just missed it. For instance, Amos 8:7–10 reads, *"Now the LORD has sworn this oath by his own mane . . . 'I will never forget the wicked things you have done! The earth will tremble for your deeds, and everyone will mourn. . . . At that time . . . I will make the sun go down at noon and darken the earth while it is still day.*

"'I will turn your celebrations into times of mourning, and your songs of joy will be turned into weeping. You will wear funeral cloths and shave your heads as signs of sorrow, as if your only son had died. How very bitter that day will be!'" This speaks of the way Jesus died on the cross.

Psalm 89:25–26 reads, *"I will extend his rule from the Mediterranean Sea in the west to the Tigris and Euphrates rivers in the east. And he will say to me, 'You are my Father, my God, and the Rock of my salvation.'"* Everyone knows that Jesus is our Rock!

Isaiah 43:10–11 tells us this about God's person Jesus: *"But you are my witnesses, O Israel!' says the* L*ORD*. *'And you are my servant. You have been chosen to know me, believe in me, and understand that I alone am God. There is no other God; there never has been and never will be. I am the* L*ORD* . . ."'

Jesus, as the Savior, is the only one of God's persons who can save us. For this reason, we should not look to people to for salvation. Nor should we look to organizations, philosophies, slogans, rules and regulations, or anything else that may come from the minds of men. These things can't help us. Only Christ can. Men cannot guarantee that we will be alive even for the next minute.[7]

What's more, Jesus, the Son, is the only person of the Godhead who relates to us on a personal, human level. This is why He is called our personal Savior. That is to say, He came as one of us, in human flesh. If He had come any other way, we would never have been able to identify with Him as one of our own. Then God would have forever been just an abstract thought to us, and not someone we could feel and touch with our own hands.[8]

At the same time, God will never confuse us with three different sources (sets) of instructions. The Father, the first person of the Godhead, is always the source of everything God says and does. Namely, He is the distinct person of the Godhead who directs the affairs of God. This keeps things from becoming disorganized.[9]

Jesus confirmed this when He said to the Father, *"I brought glory to you here on earth by doing everything you told me to do. And now, Father, bring me into the glory we shared before the world began. I have told these men about you. They were in the world, but then you gave them to me. Actually, they were always yours, and you gave them to me; and they have kept your word. Now they know that everything I have is a gift from you, for I have passed on to them the words you gave me; and they accepted them and know that I came from you, and they believe you sent me"* (John 17:4–8).

Earlier Jesus had said to the Jews: *"If anyone hears me and doesn't obey me, I am not his judge—for I have come to save the world and not to judge it. But all who reject me and my message will be judged at the . . . [Day of Judgment] by the truth I have spoken. I don't speak on my own authority. The Father who sent me gave me his own instructions as to what I should say. And I know his instructions lead to eternal life; so I say whatever the Father tells me to say!"* (John 12:47–50).

This makes the Son the dwelling place of the Father, and the Father the dwelling place of the Son. Another way to say this is, the Son is where the Father lives and the Father is where the Son lives. This is what Jesus meant when He prayed to the Father: "I have given them the glory you gave me, so that they may be one, as we are—I in them and you in me. . . . Then the world will know that you sent me and will understand that you love them as much as you love me" (John 17:22–23).[10]

Jesus told the Jews in John 10:25–30, *"I have already told you, and you don't believe me. The proof is what I do in the name of my Father. But you don't believe me because you are not part of my flock. My sheep recognize my voice; I know them, and they follow me. I give them eternal life, and they will never perish. No one can snatch them away from me, for my Father has given them to me, and he is more powerful than anyone else. So no one can take them from me. The Father and I are one."*

The Holy Spirit is God's third person. As such, He is the way God helps His people to understand His words, and what He wants them to do. An example is seen in Acts 16:6–8: *"Next Paul and Silas traveled through the area of Phrygia and Galatia, because the Holy Spirit had told them not to go into the province of Asia at that time. Then coming to the borders of Mysia, they headed for the province of Bithynia, but again the Spirit of Jesus did not let them go. So instead, they went on through Mysia to the city of Troas."*

But I must point out that these were not audible words like those Jesus spoke when He was on earth! The Holy Spirit reveals, shows, and gives us impressions directly into our spirits!

We could say the Holy Spirit motivates us to act for God. By this, I mean that His power is so great that He can stir us to action or move us to act in the way God wants us to. This is what Paul is telling us. And this is what God wants us to understand about His Spirit. Also, the Holy Spirit goes before God's preachers and prepares the way for them. What I am saying is before we stand to speak, oftentimes the Holy Spirit has already prepared the hearts of the people to receive what we are saying. We call this "convicting us of sin."

We see an example of the convicting work of the Holy Spirit by what happened to Lydia in Acts 16. As Paul preached along the riverbank, the Holy Spirit worked on Lydia's heart. Then she believed the Gospel Paul was preaching and was saved. It could have happened in no other way.

"On the Sabbath we went a little way outside the city to a riverbank, where we supposed that some people met for prayer, and we sat down to speak with some women who had come together," Luke tells us. *"One of them was Lydia from Thyatira, a merchant of expensive purple cloth. She was a worshiper of God. As she listened to us, the Lord opened her heart, and she accepted what Paul was saying. She was baptized along with other members of her household, and she asked us to be her guests. 'If you agree that I am faithful to the Lord,' she said, 'come and stay at my home.' And she urged us until we did"* (Acts 16:13–15).

If the Holy Spirit is not acting upon a person's heart, the Gospel will not be understood, no matter how cleverly it is presented. The sinful mind is just not in tune with the things of God, and never will be (Romans 8:7; 1 Corinthians 2:14). This is why we see many people reading the Bible, but without the benefit of the Spirit; what they read remains a mystery to them, and they never become saved. As a result, we see the church filled with unsaved people. Even many ministers who preach to the people are in this state (Acts 19:1–7).

I personally have seen this many times. I have seen people read the Bible and have no clue as to what they read. Or they come up with totally outlandish conclusions. I saw one man read Habakkuk 3:3 and come to the conclusion that God lives in Teman, or that God came from Teman, when this clearly is not what God meant. This verse is speaking figuratively about the land of Edom and how God will deal with its sins.

Below are some other ways the Holy Spirit helps us:

- He helps us to have self-control
- He helps think about Jesus
- He helps us love our neighbor
- He gives us peace and joy
- He gives us faith
- He gives us the power to live for God

Also, the Holy Spirit gives us the power to reject unbiblical messages. Paul pronounced a curse on anyone who would present an unbiblical message. *"Let God's curse fall on anyone, including myself, who preaches any other message than the one we told you about. Even if an angel comes from heaven and preaches any other message, let him be forever cursed. I will say it again: If anyone preached any other gospel than the one you welcomed, let God's curse fall upon that person"* (Galatians 1:8–9).

Jesus tells us in the book of Jeremiah, *". . . can you name even one of these prophets who knows the LORD well enough to hear what he is saying? Has even one of them cared enough to listen? Look! The LORD's anger bursts out like a storm, a whirlwind that swirls down on the heads of the wicked. The anger of the LORD will not diminish until it has finished all his plans. In the days to come, you will understand all this very clearly.*

"'I have not sent these prophets, yet they claim to speak for me. I have given them no message, yet they prophesy'" (Jeremiah 23:18–21).

This means that the Holy Spirit will not lead us to engage in wild speculations about people's future!

Paul told Timothy in 1 Timothy 1:3–9:

When I left for Macedonia, I urged you to stay there in Ephesus and stop those who are teaching wrong doctrine. Don't let people waste time in endless speculations over myths and spiritual pedigrees. For these things only cause arguments; they don't help people to live a life of faith in God. The purpose of my instruction is that all the Christians there would be filled with love that comes from a pure heart, a clear conscious and sincere faith. But some teachers have missed this whole point. They have turned away from these things and spend their time arguing and talking foolishness. They want to be known as teachers of the . . . [Law] of Moses, but they don't know what they are talking about, even though they seen so confident. We know these laws are good when they are used as God intended. But they were not made for people who do what is right. They are for people who are disobedient and rebellious, who are ungodly and sinful, who consider nothing sacred and defile what is holy, who murder their father or mother or other people.

The same can be said about the other foolish messages we hear today. Jude tells us to *"contend for the faith which was once delivered to the saints"* (Jude 3–4, KJV). But the "faith" or message that was "once delivered" to these early saints is the message about the person of Jesus and His death on the cross. In other words, it is the message about how the Father (the first person of the Godhead) sent the Son (the second person of the Godhead) into the world to die to free us from sin.

At this point, let's say definitely how Jesus, the Son, is God. He is the way God has revealed Himself to us. He is the way God speaks to us. He is the way God died on the cross for us. He is the way God rose from the dead for us. And He is the way God is coming back to take us to heaven at the last day. What more can we ask of God?

Jesus has always existed as the personal self-expression of the One true God. *"At the beginning God expressed himself. That personal expression, that word, was with God, and was God, and he existed with God from the beginning. All creation took place through him, and none took place without him. In him appeared life and this life was the light of mankind. The light shines in the darkness and the darkness has never put it out"* (John 1:5, NTME).

King David said this about Jesus, the Son: *"The LORD lives! Blessed be my rock! May the God of my salvation be exalted! He is the God who pays back those who harm me; he subdues the nations under me and rescues me from my enemies. You hold me safe beyond the reach of my enemies; you save me from violent opponents. For this, O LORD, I will praise you among the nations; I will sing joyfully to your name"* (Psalm 18:46–49).

Paul commented thusly: *"Christ is the one through whom God created everything in heaven and earth. He made all things we can see and things we can't see—kings, kingdoms, rulers, and authorities. Everything has been created through him and for him. He existed before everything else began, and he holds all creation together"* (Colossians 1:16–17).

The *Athanasian Creed* states: ". . . that we worship one God in three persons and three persons in one God, neither confusing the persons nor dividing the substance. [Truly,] . . . there is one person of the Father, another of the Son, and another of the Holy Spirit. But the Godhead of the Father, of the Son, and of the Holy Spirit is all one: the glory equal, the majesty coeternal. Such as the Father is, such is the Son, and such is the Holy Spirit. . . . And yet there are not . . . [Gods] but one . . . [God]. . . ." [11]

That Jesus is God is the most important revelation we can receive in these days of open idolatry. Religions from the east are flooding the Christian market with ideas of demon gods and goddesses, witches, and warlocks. They may talk about Christ, but they present Him to us as one of many false gods. Or they present Him as weak and ineffective, having to bow to the wishes of humans.

Listen to what God said about Jesus (Isaiah 42:1–4): *"Look at my servant, whom I strengthen. He is my chosen one, and I am pleased with him. I have put my Spirit upon him. He will reveal justice to the nations. He will be gentle—he will not shout or raise his voice in public. He will not crush those who are weak or quench the smallest hope. He will bring full justice to all who have been wronged.*

"He will not stop until truth and righteousness prevail throughout the earth. Even distant lands beyond the sea will wait on his instructions."

Didn't Jesus do all these things when He was on earth? And doesn't this prove He is God? Plus, Jesus healed the sick, raised the dead, gave sight to the blind, and made the cripple walk. He did many more miracles that I will not list here. What more do we want from Him?

To summarize the workings of the Trinity, the Father gives instructions; the Son carries them out by speaking and acting for God, and the Holy Spirit gives us the power to believe in what we are seeing. In other words, He helps us to believe in what God is saying and doing through Jesus.

This is proven by what Jesus, the Son, said in John 5:20: *"For the Father loves the Son and tells him everything he is doing, and the Son will do far greater things than healing this man. You will be astonished at what he does."* We see another example in John 5:30. Here, Jesus tells us, *"But I do nothing without consulting the Father. I judge as I am told. And my judgment is absolutely just, because it is according to the will of God who sent me; it is not merely my own."*

He said in John 16:14–15: *"He [the Spirit] will bring me glory by revealing to you whatever he receives from me. All that the Father has is mine; this is what I mean when I say the Spirit will reveal to you whatever he receives from me."*

Luke tells us in Acts 13:1–3, *"Among the prophets and teachers of the church at Antioch of Syria were Barnabas, Simeon (called 'the Black man'), Lucius (from Cyrene), Manaen (the childhood companion of King Herod Antipas), and Saul. One day as these men were worshiping the Lord and fasting, the Holy Spirit said, 'Dedicate Barnabas and Saul for the special work I have for them.' So after more fasting and prayer, the men laid their hands on them and sent them on their way."*

We see further proof of this in John 14:15–26. In verse 16, Jesus told His disciples, *"And I will ask the Father, and he will give you another Counselor [the Holy Spirit], who will never leave you."* Then in verse 18, when speaking of His role as the Son in the Godhead, He told them, *"No, I will not abandon you as orphans—I will come to you."* And in verse 23, when speaking of His relationship with the Father, He said, *"And we will come to them and live with them."* How could all three of the members of the Godhead come to live in us and share in our development if they are not acting in unison?

This is why the Jews endeavored to stone Jesus for blasphemy. They understood Jesus' claim to be the "Son of God" as a claim that put Him on the same level with God. To them, such a thing was unthinkable.

There is much we do not know about God, however. Furthermore, no human can ever be Jesus, the Son of God. Such a thing is utterly impossible. Any teaching along this line is utter nonsense (1 Corinthians 1:20). It is complete heresy and has no place in the Christian Church.

Many misunderstand the words of Jesus that say, *"It is written in your own law that God said to certain leaders of the people, 'I say, you are gods!' And you know that the Scriptures cannot be altered. So if those people, who received God's message, were called 'gods,' why do you call it blasphemy when the Holy One who was sent into the world by the Father says, 'I am the Son of God'?"* (John 10:34–36). They think that Jesus was talking about us today, as we become more righteous. But this is a complete misunderstanding of what Jesus was saying, and has led to much confusion.

In this Scripture, Jesus was using an analogy (parable) to show the people that many of those who held important positions in the Jewish community were often thought of as "gods" because they were permitted to judge the people. But in reality (in God's sight), they were not gods at all. However, if the people they judged were willing to look upon them as gods, then Jesus reasoned that they shouldn't have any problem believing that He, the One the Father sent into the world, was God.

Also, Jesus never said that these judges existed from eternity past, as the Almighty does (Revelation 1:8). And He surely did not say they had "all power," as He does (Matthew 28:18). He only said that they were allowed to judge the people of Israel and rule them by the will of God (John 19:11).

The fact that false Christs would appear can be seen by what Jesus said in Matthew 24: *"For many will come in my name, saying, 'I am the Messiah.' They will lead many astray.... And many will turn away from me and betray and hate each other. And many false prophets will appear and will lead many people astray. Sin will be rampant everywhere, and the love of many will grow cold. But those who endure to the end will be saved"* (Matthew 24:5–13).

He tells us in verses 23–28: *"Then if anyone tells you, 'Look, here is the Messiah,' or 'There he is,' don't pay any attention. For false messiahs and false prophets will rise up and perform great miraculous signs and wonders so as to deceive, if possible, even God's chosen ones. See, I have warned you.*

"So if someone tells you, 'Look, the Messiah is out in the desert,' don't bother to go and look. Or, 'Look, he is hiding here,' don't believe it! For as the lightning lights up the entire sky, so it will be when the Son of man comes. Just as the gathering of vultures shows [us] there is a carcass nearby, so these signs indicate that the end is near" (Matthew 24:23–28).

I will conclude this chapter by saying this: God is one God, but in these last days, Jesus is the way He speaks to us. This makes Jesus the only way to heaven. If we reject Jesus, then we can have no salvation.

---

1 "Isaiah 45:21—Passage Lookup—King James Version . . .," p. 1, http://www.biblegateway.com/passage/?search=Isaiah+45%3A21&version=KJV; Internet; accessed 16 September 2009.

2 "The Trinity—A short exposition by Francis J. Beckwith," pp. 1–6, http://www.answering-islam.org/Trinity/beckwith.html; Internet; accessed 18 August 2009.

3 "declare," <u>Merriam-Webster's Online Dictionary</u>, pp. 1–2, http://www.merriam-webster.com/dictionary/declare; Internet; accessed 17 September 2009.

4 "John 14:9—Passage Lookup—New International Version . . .," p. 1, http://www.biblegateway.com/passage/?search=John+14%3A9&version=NIV; Internet; accessed 17 September 2009.

5 "Explain the Trinity—Holy Trinity—Trinity Doctrine," pp. 1–2, http://www.everystudent.com/forum/trinity.html; Internet; accessed 14 March 2010.

6 "The Trinity (Triunity) of God . . .," pp. 1–16, http://bible.org/article/trinity-triunity-god; Internet; accessed 19 August 2009.

7 "Acts 4:12—Passage Lookup—New International Version . . .," p. 1, http://www.biblegateway.com/passage/?search=Acts+4%3A12&version=NIV; Internet; accessed 18 September 2009.

8 "Hebrews 2:17—Passage Lookup—New International Version . . .," p. 1, http://www.biblegateway.com/passage/?search=Hebrews+2%3A17&version=NIV; Internet; accessed 18 September 2009.

9 "John 20:21—Passage Lookup—New International Version . . .," p. 1, <http;//www.biblegateway.com/passage/?search=John+20%3A21&version=NIV>; Internet; accessed 17 September 2009.

10 "John 14:11–12—Passage Lookup—New international Version . . .," p. 1, http://www.biblegateway.com/passage/?search=John+14%11-12&version=NIV; Internet; accessed 18 September 2009.

11 "Athanasian Creed . . .," pp. 1–3, http://www.lcms.org/pages/internal.asp?NavID=3357; Internet; accessed 14 March 2010.

9

CHRIST IN EZEKIEL'S WHEEL

In his famous vision by the river Kebar in Babylon, the prophet Ezekiel saw a vision of wheels turning in the air, accompanied by four living beings, above which sat the figure of a man. To top it off, this all seemed to be one object or structure. This was a vision of Jesus in all His splendor and glory.

Let's began our study in Ezekiel 1:4: *"As I looked, I saw a great storm coming toward me from the north, driving before it a huge cloud that flashed with lightning and shone with brilliant light. The fire inside the cloud glowed like a gleaming amber."*

This brings to mind the glory God displayed when He appeared to the Jews on Mt. Sinai. God said to Moses that He would appear to the people in a cloud so thick the people could hardly bear it. Then on the day of His appearing, there was a great thunderstorm, filled with lightning. Then a long blast from a ram's horn was heard, making the people tremble (Exodus 19). This displayed God's power, making sure the viewers knew it was Him. The same is taking place here.

Let's say it this way. God is all powerful, and He often uses elements of His creation to display this power. This speaks of Him as Creator and displays the fame, admiration, and honor that belong to Him, evidencing His glory. Wouldn't you do this if you were God?

Romans 1:19–20 says it like this: *"For the truth about God is known to them instinctively. God has put this knowledge in their hearts. From the time the world was created, people have seen the earth and the sky and all that God made. They can clearly see his invisible qualities—his eternal power and divine nature. . . ."*

Jeremiah 31:35–35 says, *"It is the LORD who provides the sun to light the day and the moon and stars to light the night. It is he who stirs the sea into roaring waves. His name is the LORD Almighty, and this is what he says: 'I am as likely to reject my people*

Israel as I am to do away with the laws of nature!'"

In verses 5–9 Ezekiel sees four living beings: *"From the center of the cloud came four living beings that looked human, except that each had four faces and two pairs of wings. Their legs were straight like human legs, but their feet were split like calves' feet and shone like burnished bronze. Beneath each of their wings I could see human hands. The wings of each living being touched the wings of the two beings beside it. The living beings were able to fly in any direction without turning around."*

Verse 10 states, *"Each had a human face in the front, the face of a lion on the right side, the face of an ox on the left side, and the face of an eagle at the back."*

This, too, displays God's glory. But more importantly, it displays a truth about God that very few recognize. Notice that each of the beings had four faces!

The first face was the face of a human, picturing Jesus as the "Son of Man" (Matthew 26:31). As a man, then, Jesus came and died a physical death for the sins of us all. This was the only death God would accept. In other words, it was a man who sinned, thus, it was a man who had to die for sin.

The second face was that of a lion. This pictures Jesus as the lion of the tribe of Judah. Jesus says of Himself in this role, *"I will come like a lion from the thickets of the Jordan, leaping on the sheep in the pasture. I will chase Babylon from its land, and I will appoint the leader of my choice. For who is like me, and who can challenge me? What ruler can oppose my will?"*

Jacob made reference to Jesus in this mode in Genesis 40:8–10 when he said, *"Judah, your brothers will praise you. You will defeat your enemies. All your relatives will bow before you. Judah is a young lion that has finished eating its prey. Like a lion he crouches and lies down; like a lioness—who will dare to rouse him? The scepter will not depart from Judah, nor the ruler's staff from his descendants, until the coming of the one to whom it belongs, the one whom all nations will obey."*

The third face was that of an eagle. An eagle is a bird of prey, but it is also a defender of its young. Jesus says of those He protects: *"But they that wait on the LORD will find new strength. They will fly high on wings like eagles. They will run and not get weary. They will walk and not faint"* (Isaiah 41:31). Revelation 12:13–14 states: *"And when the dragon realized that he had been thrown down to the earth, he pursued the woman who had given birth to the child. But she was given two wings like those of a great eagle. This allowed her to fly to a place prepared for her in the wilderness, where she would be cared for and protected from the dragon for a time, times, and half a time."*

The fourth face was that of an ox. An ox has great strength. It was used in the Jewish sacrifice of the burnt offering. "If your sacrifice for a whole burnt offering is from the herd, bring a bull with no physical defects to the entrance of the Tabernacle so it will be accepted by the LORD. Lay your hand on its head so the LORD will accept it as your substitute thus making atonement for you. All Bible scholars know this is a picture of Jesus, i.e., our substitute.

We could say, then, that the four faces represent four aspects of Jesus, as He works out the salvation of the world. In other words, as Jesus saves us, we see Him in the Scriptures as a man, a furious lion, a protecting eagle, and a strong, yet submissive ox.

The straight legs indicate that Jesus, while on earth, walked uprightly, straight in the path of the Gospel He preached. We could say that He walked in no crooked path, or turned to the right or left. And once He set His "hand to the plough," He did not turn back.

Calves feet, round and with a divided hoof, are perfect for providing balance as the calf does his work. So it is with Jesus. He is strong and perfectly balanced as He preaches the Gospel of salvation and predicts judgment for those who reject it. We too, as ministers of Jesus, should be this way. We should preach exactly what Jesus preached, and not be afraid to tell people about their sins or the fires of hell. Ephesians 6:15–16 says it this way: *"For shoes, put on the peace that comes from the Good News, so that you will be fully prepared. In every battle you will need faith as your shield to stop the fiery arrows aimed at you by Satan."*

Human hands picture work. This pictures Christ as always doing God's work on earth. That is, He is always actively doing the will of God. He said of Himself in John 5:29–30, *". . . and they will rise again. Those who have done good will rise to eternal life, and those who have continued in evil will rise to judgment. But I do nothing without consulting the Father. I judge as I am told. And my judgment is absolutely just, because it is accordingly to the will of God who sent me; it is not merely my own."*

Verses 11–12 of Ezekiel 1 read: *"Each had two pairs of outstretched wings—one pair stretched out to touch the wings of the living beings on either side of it, and the other pair covered its body. They went in whatever direction the spirit chose, and they moved straight forward in all directions without having to turn around."*

The two pairs of wings depict Jesus as the God of both the Old Testament and the New Testament. He is the "I Am" who gave the law (Exodus 20), and the "But I say" who defined the law's end and the coming of grace in the New Testament (Matthew 5:28). The last part of these verses can be interpreted, "God goes in whatever direction He chooses to, and He saves us in whatever way He desires." This means that the law had its purpose, but now God's grace is all we need.

The two wings that covered the beings' bodies picture the same thing; Jesus is covered with the Gospel of grace, but fulfills it in the light of God's law!

Verses 13–14 of Ezekiel 1 read: *"The living beings looked like bright coals of fire or brilliant torches, and it looked as though lightning was flashing back and forth among them. And the living beings darted to and fro like flashes of lightning."*

This pictures Jesus as the burning coal who burns away our sins. That is to say, He is the One who removes our sins by His atoning sacrifice: *"Then one of the seraphim flew over to the altar, and he picked up a burning coal with a pair of* tongs. He touched my lips with it and said, 'See, this coal has touched your lips. Now your guilt is removed, and your sins are forgiven'" (Isaiah 6:5–7).

Numbers 16:46 says it like this: *"And Moses said to Aaron, 'Quick, take an incense burner and place burning coals on it from the altar. Lay incense on it and carry it quickly among the people to make atonement for them. . . .'"*

About the living beings darting to and fro like flashes of lightning, lightning pictures Jesus as the light of the world. Psalm 27:13 reads: *"The LORD is my light and my salvation—so why should I be afraid? The LORD protects me from danger—so why should I tremble? When evil people come to destroy me, when my enemies and foes attack me, they will stumble and fall. Though a mighty army surrounds me, my heart will know no fear. Even if they attack me, I remain confident."*

Lightning also pictures the return of Jesus: *"'So if someone tells you, "Look, the Messiah is out in the desert," don't bother to go and look. Or, "Look, he is hiding here," don't believe it! For as the lightning lights up the entire sky, so it will be when the Son of Man comes. Just as the . . . vultures shows there is a carcass nearby, so these signs indicate that the end is near'"* (Matthew 24:26–28).

Now to the verses of even more interest (Ezekiel 1:15–18): *"As I looked at these beings, I saw four wheels on the ground beneath them, and one wheel belonging to each. The wheels sparkled as if made of chrysolite [gem stones]. All four wheels looked the same; each wheel had a second wheel turning crosswise within it.*

"The beings could move forward in any of the four directions they faced, without turning as they moved. The rims of the four wheels were awesomely tall, and they were covered with eyes all around the edges."

When we think about it, it takes four wheels to make up the foundation of one chariot. And that's what the prophet saw, the one chariot of God going to and fro, carrying Jesus about to oversee His domain.

The prophet Zechariah saw four chariots in his vision, indicating that God's chariot covers the four corners of the earth: *"Then I looked up again and saw four chariots coming from between two bronze mountains. The first chariot was pulled by red horses, the second by black horses, the third by white horses, and the fourth by dappled-grey horses. 'And what are these, my lord?' I asked the angel who was talking with me.*

"He replied, 'These are the four spirits of heaven who stand before the Lord of all the earth. They are going out to do his work. . . .' The powerful horses were eager to be off, to patrol back and forth across the earth. And the LORD said, 'Go and patrol the earth!' So they left at once on their patrol" (Zechariah 6:1–7).

All the wheels of the chariot looked the same because God is the same. *"Jesus Christ is the same yesterday, today, and forever. So do not be attracted by strange, new ideas. Your spiritual strength comes from God's special favor, not from ceremonial rules about food, which don't help those who follow them."* (Hebrews 13:8–9).

The wheels are a picture of Jesus moving under the power of God.

He is God. The wheel turning within each wheel is Jesus too. We could say it this way: Everything revolves around Him; He makes the world go and is the cetnral feature of everything God does.

The fact that the wheels were covered with eyes means that God sees all we do and responds accordingly!

Verses 19–21 of Ezekiel 1 read: *"When the four living beings moved, the wheels moved with them. When they flew upward, the wheels went up, too. The spirit of the four living beings was in the wheels. So wherever the spirit went, the wheels and the living beings went, too. When the living beings moved, the wheels moved. When the living beings stopped, the wheels stopped. When the living beings flew into the air, the wheels rose up. For the spirit of the living beings was in the wheels."*

All of this points to the fact that God is one, that is, He is one Spirit. 2 Corinthians 3:16–18 reads, *"But whenever anyone turns to the Lord, then the veil is taken away. Now, the Lord is the Spirit, and wherever the Spirit of the Lord is, he gives freedom. And all of us have had that veil removed so that we can be mirrors that brightly reflect the glory of the Lord. And as the Spirit of the Lord works within us, we become more and more like him and reflect his glory even more."*

Verses 22–28 of Ezekiel 1 read: *"There was a surface spread out above them like the sky. . . . Above the surface over their heads was what looked like a throne made of . . . [blue jewels]. And high above this throne was a figure whose appearance was like that of a man. From his waist up, he looked like gleaming amber, flickering like fire. And from the waist down, he looked like a burning flame, shining with splendor. All around him was a glowing halo, like a rainbow shining through the clouds. This was the way the glory of the* LORD *appeared to me. When I saw it, I fell down in the dust and I heard someone's voice speaking to me."*

This is a reference to the way John saw Jesus on the Island of Patmos (Revelation 1:12– 16): *"When I turned to see who was speaking to me, I saw seven gold lampstands. And standing in the middle of the lampstands was the Son of Man. He was wearing a long robe with a gold sash across his chest. His head and his hair were white like wool, as white as snow.*

"And his eyes were bright like flames of fire. His feet were as bright as bronze refined in a furnace, and his voice thundered like mighty ocean waves. He held seven stars in his right hand, and a sharp two-edged sword came from his mouth. And his face was as bright as the sun in its brilliance."

There is one quandary that needs to be cleared up, however. In Ezekiel 10:9, the prophet referred to the four living beings as cherubim. But then he said in verse 15: *". . . These were the same living beings I had seen beside the Kebar River."* What is he trying to tell us?

Oftentimes Jesus appeared in the Old Testament as an angel. He did this to present Himself to us as God's messenger. But this in no way detracts from His distinction as being God, or from His glory as God. Jesus can appear to us in any way He wants to.

Didn't Jacob wrestle with an angel who turned out to be God? *"Before Jacob was born, he struggled with his brother; when he became a man he even fought with God. Yes, he wrestled with the angel and won. He wept and pleaded for a blessing from him. There at Bethel he met God face to face, and God spoke to him—the* LORD *God Almighty is his name!"* (Hosea 12:3–5).

We can sum Ezekiel's vision like this: Ezekiel's vision is a picture of Christ in all His glory. It was God's way of identifying Himself as the sovereign Lord—the Lord God Almighty, the coming Savior of the world. This agrees with what the Bible says about the Old Testament prophets: *"This salvation was something the prophets wanted to know more about. They prophesied about this gracious salvation prepared for you, even though they had many questions as to what it all could mean.*

"They wondered what the Spirit of Christ within them was talking about when he told them in advance about Christ's suffering and his great glory afterward. They wondered when and to whom all this would happen" (1 Peter 1:10–11).

The old Negro spiritual says it like this:

Ezek'el saw the wheel
'Way up in the middle o' the air
Ezek'el saw the wheel
'Way in the middle o' the air
The big wheel moved by faith
The little wheel moved by the grace o' God
A wheel in a wheel
'Way in the middle o' the air
Jes' let me tell you what a hypocrite'll do
'Way in the middle o' the air
He'll talk about me an' he'll talk about you
'Way in the middle o' the air
Watch out my sister how you walk on the cross
'Way in the middle o' the air
Yo' foot might slip an' yo' soul get lost
'Way in the middle o' the air
You say the Lord has set you free
'Way in the middle o' the air
Why don't you let your neighbor be?
'Way in the middle o' the air
(Ezek'el [Ezekiel] Saw the Wheel)[1]

---

1 "... (Ezekiel) Saw the Wheel...," pp. 1–2, 26, http://www.negrospirituals.com/news-song/zekiel_ezekiel_saw_the_wheel.htm; Internet; accessed 26 July 2011.

10

COMPLETE IN CHRIST: THE FINAL BLESSING

The old saints had a saying: "Jesus is all I need." In reference to this, they would sing the following lyrics:

> Jesus is all . . . [this] world to me,
> My life, my joy, my all;
> He is my strength from day to day,
> Without Him I would fall.
> When I am sad, to Him I go,
> No other one can cheer me so;
> When I am sad, He makes me glad,
> He's my Friend.
> Jesus is all . . . [this] world to me,
> My Friend in trials sore;
> I go to Him for blessings, and
> He gives them o'er and o'er.
> He sends the sunshine and the rain,
> He sends the harvest's golden grain;
> Sunshine and rain, harvest of grain,
> He's my Friend.
> (First two stanzas, "Jesus Is All the World to Me," Will L. Thompson, 1904)[1]

The Scripture reference for this song is 2 Peter 1:3–4: *"As we know Jesus better, his divine power gives us everything we need for living a godly life. He has called us to receive his own glory and goodness! And by that same mighty power, he has given us all of his rich and wonderful promises. He has promised that you will escape the decadence all around you caused by evil desires and that you will share in his divine nature."*

Philippians 4:18–19 reads: *"At the moment I have all I need—more than I need! I am generously supplied with the gifts you sent me with Epaphroditus. They are a sweet-smelling sacrifice that is acceptable to God and pleases him. And this same God who takes care of me will supply all your needs from his glorious riches, which have been given to us in Christ Jesus."*

These are true statements and always will be. The problem is we take our eyes off what Jesus is actually offering us, that is, salvation and a home in heaven. Nothing in this world can make Him not deliver on these promises!

Speaking of Jesus, David observed: *"Open for me the gates where the righteous enter . . . I will go in and thank the LORD. Those gates lead to the presence of the LORD, and the godly enter there. I thank you for answering my prayer and saving me!*

"The stone rejected by the builders has now become the . . . [foundation stone]. This is the LORD's doing, and it is marvelous to see. This is the day the LORD has made. We will rejoice and be glad in it. Please, LORD, please save us" (Psalm 118:19–25).

If we are sincere about going to heaven, we must put our trust in Jesus. Jesus tells us in John 12:27–28: *"My Father has given me authority over everything. No one really knows the Son except the Father, and no one really knows the Father except the Son and those to whom the Son chooses to reveal him.*

"Come to me, all of you who are weary and carry heavy burdens, and I will give you rest."

Colossians 3:1–4 states: *"Since you have been raised to new life with Christ, set your sights on the realities of heaven, where Christ sits at God's right hand in the place of honor and power. Let heaven fill your thoughts. Do not think only about things down here on earth. For you died when Christ died, and your real life is hidden with Christ in God. And when Christ, who is your real life, is revealed to the whole world, you will share in all his glory."*

But what about getting more of the Spirit? Doesn't that make us better Christians?

If you are saved, you have all the Spirit you will ever need. The Holy Spirit cannot be given out in small doses. As we have learned, God is one entity and always will be one entity. Those who teach that He is not are confused about what the Scriptures teach. I, myself, used to think along these lines before I allowed Jesus to teach me. Hopefully, after reading this book, many others will be able to say the same thing.

But some may still ask, "What about what happened on the Day of Pentecost? Didn't these people receive more of God's Spirit?" The answer is no! They didn't have the Holy Spirit living in them at this time. He was only with them. But now God deposited His Spirit directly into their souls, making then entirely new people. He does the same for us.

We see the same thing repeated at the conversion of Cornelius and his household (Acts 10:44–47): *"Even as Peter was saying these things, the Holy Spirit fell upon all who had heard the message. The Jewish believers who came with Peter were amazed that the gift of the Holy Spirit had been poured out upon the Gentiles, too. And there could be no doubt about it, for they heard them speaking in tongues and praising God.*

"Then Peter asked, 'Can anyone object to their being baptized now that they have received the Holy Spirit just as we did?'"

Peter verified this when he said in Acts 15:8–9, *"God, who knows people's hearts, confirmed that he accepts Gentiles by giving them the Holy Spirit, just as he gave him to us. He made no distinction between us and them, for he also cleansed their hearts through faith."*

Notice that Peter said that God made no distinction between the first followers of Jesus and the Gentiles who were now being saved. If the disciples in the upper room received a "full measure" of the Spirit, then Cornelius and his followers did too.

It is also seen after Philip's preaching in Samaria: *"When the apostles back in Jerusalem heard that the people of Samaria had accepted God's message, they sent Peter and John there. As soon as they arrived they prayed for these new Christians to receive the Holy Spirit. The Holy Spirit had not yet come upon any of them, for they had only been baptized in the name of the Lord Jesus. Then Peter and John laid their hands upon these believers, and they received the Holy Spirit"* (Acts 8:14–17).

We see a type of God giving us His Spirit in the days of Noah: *"When the human population began to grow rapidly on the earth, the sons of God saw the beautiful women of the human race and took any they wanted as their wives. Then the LORD said, 'My Spirit will not put up with humans for such a long time for they are only mortal flesh . . .'"* (Genesis 6:1–3).

Many scholars believe that the sons of God mentioned here is a reference to fallen angels. But this is not the case. Angels are composed of Spirit, and therefore, cannot marry into the human race. If they could, we would see evidence of it today.

Furthermore, God never gave His Spirit to angels, or to any supposed offspring of angels. The Spirit of God is reserved only for the human race. We are the only ones of God's creation He saves in this way. God promised us this in Joel 2:28–29: *"Then after I have poured out my rains again, I will pour out my Spirit upon all people. Your sons and daughters will prophecy. Your old men will dream dreams. Your young men will see visions. In those days, I will pour out my Spirit even on servants, men and women alike.'"*

Then to prove His point, God said in verses 30–32: *"I will cause wonders in the heavens and on the earth—blood and fire and pillars of smoke. The sun will be turned into darkness, and the moon will turn blood red before that great and terrible day of the LORD arrives. And anyone who calls on the name of the LORD will be saved. . . ."*

We see God giving His Spirit to Samson as a type: *"As Samson and his parents were going down to Timnah, a young lion attacked Samson near the vineyards of Timnah. At that moment the Spirit of the* LORD *powerfully took control of him, and he ripped the lion's jaws apart with his bare hands. He did it as easily as if it were a young goat . . ."* (Judges 14:5–6).

This speaks of how Samson did great feats by God's Spirit. Later he would defeat the Philistines by this same power. This is a type of how the Holy Spirit will give us power to overcome our desires to commit overt sins. We can be changed into a new person too. We can be changed into a person who loves Jesus, and one who has the desire to serve Him to the fullest. Thank God for the Holy Spirit.

But let me say this before I move on. It is Jesus who gives us the Holy Spirit. The Holy Spirit is not attained any other way. The Holy Spirit cannot be attained by fasting, praying, doing good deeds, etc. If so, there would be no need for Jesus.

Many people try this approach anyway. They think that by intensive concentration they can work themselves into a holy state. Or that the Holy Spirit will notice their desire for Him and show Himself. Others engage in wild emotional episodes. Some go so far as to lose consciousness or enter an altered state of mind. Others run or dance. Some fall on the floor. Some even attempt to buy God's Spirit. But these things do not work. They may make us feel good about ourselves or make us believe that something has taken place, but they are not signs of God's Spirit. God's Spirit comes only from trusting Jesus to save us.

The prophet Micah said it like this: *"This is what the* LORD *says to you false prophets: 'You are leading my people astray! You promise peace for those who give you food, but you declare war on anyone who refuses to pay you. Now the night will close around you, cutting off all your visions. . . .'*

"But as for me, I am filled with power and the Spirit of the LORD. *I am filled with justice and might, fearlessly pointing out Israel's sin and rebellion"* (Micah 3:5–8).

Look at what Jesus said to those who refused to listen to Him in the days of the prophet Isaiah. *"Destruction is certain for my rebellious children. You make plans that are contrary to my will. You weave a web of plans that are not from my Spirit, thus piling up your sins. For without consulting with me, you have gone down to Egypt to find help. You have put your trust in Pharaoh for his protection"* (Isaiah 30:1–2).

Egypt is a type for Sin. God set it us this way to prove this very point. Pharaoh, then, becomes a type for Satan, who wants to keep us in sin. But the point is that God brings us out of sin by the power of His Spirit, and He freely gives His Spirit to those who trust in Him.

But some will ask, "Doesn't God's Spirit inspire us to prophesy and know the future?" The answer is no!

If Jesus wanted us to know tiny details about the future, He would have placed our names in the Scriptures and surrounded them with such details. But He did not do this. What He did was to give us the facts that apply to all Christian's lives; we are sinners and are on our way to hell if we do not cry out to Him to save us.

The Holy Spirit inspires us to seek Jesus daily. He inspires us to pray and do Bible study. But He does not tell us about the lives of people we don't know. Yes, I see preachers doing this, but they could not be doing it by God's power. God does not operate this way.

Our mission is to preach the Gospel to people. And as Jesus said, those who believe and are saved will show their faith by being baptized. Then after people are saved, we are to instruct them in the ways of God and how to relate to their fellow Christians. This is the only duty assigned to God's people. To stray away from this is to miss the mark and subject ourselves to unwanted influences.

God's ministers should not act like mediums. Such activity is forbidden: *"Do not rely on mediums and psychics, for you will be defiled by them. I, the Lord, am your God"* (Leviticus 19:31). *"Men and women among you who act as mediums or physics must be put to death by stoning. They are guilty of a capital offense"* (Leviticus 21:27).

Now the administration of these Old Testament laws is no longer binding on God's people; that is, we can't tell people what to do or punish them for not doing it. But you see the point. Such a thing was an offense to God because He knew it was of Satan and his demons. If it was of God, God would have never condemned it. Also, if it was of God, He would have clearly commanded it in the New Testament.

The Scripture that ministers use to give "words of Knowledge" is 1 Corinthians 12:8: *"To one person the Spirit gives wise advice; to another he gives the gift of special knowledge."* But we must remember that this was before the Bible was written down for us to read. God had to communicate with His people this way or they would not have known anything. But now that the Bible is complete, and available for us to read, God no longer does this. If we insist that He still does, we are going against His will.

I am not saying that there is never an occasion when Christ will not let us display this gift. This is entirely up to God and His Divine Providence. He can open up the Red Sea, make water come out of a rock, rain down manna from heaven, roll back the Jordan River, or make the walls of Jericho fall down if He wants to. He has all power. However, for a mature believer, this sign is not necessary.

What we must do now is look to the Bible as our guide. 2 Peter 1:19–21 tells us that it was the Holy Spirit who inspired the Bible. *"Because of that, we have even greater confidence in the message proclaimed by the prophets. Pay close attention* to what they wrote, for their words are like a light shining in a dark place—until the day Christ appears and his brilliant light shines in your hearts. Above all, you must understand that no prophecy in Scripture ever came from the prophets themselves or because they wanted to prophesy. It was the Holy Spirit who moved the prophets to speak from God."

But what about our sins?

Our sins were paid for on the cross of Christ. There is no need for us to look for any other atonement: *"This is the message he has given us to announce to you: God is light and there is no darkness in him at all. So we are lying if we say we have fellowship with God but go on living in spiritual darkness. We are not living in the truth. But if we are living in the light of God's presence, just as Christ is, then we have fellowship with each other, and the blood of Jesus, his Son, cleanses us from every sin"* (1 John 1:5–8).

David acknowledged this: *"Have mercy on me, O God, because of your unfailing love. Because of your great compassion, blot out the stain of my sins. Wash me clean from my guilt. Purify me from my sin,"* he told God in Psalm 51:1–6.

"For I recognize my shameful deeds—they haunt me day and night. Against you, and you alone, have I sinned; I have done what is evil in your sight. You will be proved right in what you say, and your judgment against me is just.

"For I was born a sinner—yes, from the moment my mother conceived me. But you desire honesty from the heart, so you can teach me to be wise in my inmost being."

When Adam sinned, he sold us into the slavery of sin (Romans 7:14). As a payment for our release, the law demands our life (Ezekiel 18:4). But if we can find a substitute to die in our place, we do not have to die. This is what we see taking place on the cross. Here, we see Jesus dying in the place of every person who ever lived. It was the one for the many, the just for the unjust, the righteous for the unrighteous.

Hebrews 10:11–14 says it this way: *"Under the old covenant, the priest stands before the altar day after day, offering sacrifices that can never take away sins. But our High Priest offered himself to God as one sacrifice for sins, good for all times. Then he sat down at the place of highest honor at God's right hand. There he waits until his enemies are humbled as a footstool under his feet. For by that one offering he perfected forever all those whom he is making holy."*

What the writer is saying is God has done all He intends to do in the way of purging our sins. All we have to do is to accept it. To fight against this is to rebel against God and to tell Him that you do not believe in Him. It is also to tell Him that Jesus did not do enough on the cross, and that you want more, or that you think that you could have done a better job. This is utter nonsense.

Listen to what Isaiah 49:5–6 says about Jesus: *"And now the LORD speaks—he who formed me in my mother's womb to be his servant, who commissioned me to bring his people of Israel back to him. The LORD has honored me, and my God has given me strength. He says, 'You will do more than restore the people of Israel to me. I will make you a light to the Gentiles, and you will bring my salvation to the ends of the earth.'"*

This speaks of Jesus as the all sufficient one, the One who is able to do what He said He will do. Not only does He grant salvation to the Jews, He grants salvation to everyone else too. This was unheard of among the people who worshiped pagan gods. These gods were gods of a local tribe, or a local people. Everyone else was an enemy. They encouraged their people to fight and destroy them. But Jesus is saying that He is not like that. He loves all people, and He wants them to be saved too.

There will be people in heaven from the distant corners of the world, from places we have hardly heard of. They will come from all races, all social groups, all income levels, and all backgrounds. Many will be there that we think have no business being there. Maybe they don't meet our approval, but it makes no difference. Jesus loves them, and that is all that matters.

We tend to think that we, in America, have a corner on Jesus. But we do not. Physical blessings do not determine righteousness. If so, the Roman Empire in Paul's day would have been the most righteous nation in the world. But it was not. When Paul traveled through it, he saw decadence and evil everywhere. This is why he encountered so much hostility to the Gospel.

It continues (verse 7): *"The LORD, the Redeemer and Holy One of Israel, says to the one who is despised and rejected by a nation, to the one who is the servant of rulers: 'Kings will stand at attention when you pass by. Princes will bow low because the LORD has chosen you. He, the faithful LORD, the Holy One of Israel, chooses you.'"*

This speaks of Jesus as the KING OF KINGS AND THE LORD OF LORDS!

"Do you think . . . that I like to see wicked people die? Of course not! I only want them to turn from their wicked ways and live," Jesus said to Israel in Ezekiel 18:23.

Verses 26–28 continues: *"When righteous people turn from being good and start doing sinful things, they will die for it. Yes, they will die because of their sinful deeds. And if wicked people turn away from their wickedness, obey the law, and do what is just and right, they will save their lives. They will live, because after thinking it over, they decided to turn from their sins. Such people will not die."*

Physical goods are given to all God's children. God provides for the material needs of all of His children, even the unrighteous. Jesus said it this way: *"You have heard that the . . . [Law] of Moses says, 'Love your neighbor and hate your enemy.' But I say, love your enemies! Pray for those who persecute you! In this way you will be acting as true children of your Father in heaven. For he gives his sunlight to both the evil and the good, and he sends rain on the just and on the unjust, too. If you love only those who love you, what good is that? Even the corrupt tax collectors do that much. If you are kind only to your friends, how are you different from anyone else? Even pagans do that. But you are to be perfect, even as your Father in heaven is perfect"* (Matthew 5:43–48).

Salvation is what God's promises us under His New Covenant. We must remember, therefore, that for Paul, John the Baptist, John the Revelator, and many other of God's great saints, God's blessings were entirely spiritual. They received very little of this world's goods. But they saw and heard things of God that very few people are allowed to see and hear.

Paul told the Corinthians: *"This boasting is all so foolish, but let me go on. Let me tell about the visions and revelations I received from the Lord. I was caught up into the third heaven fourteen years ago. Whether my body was there or just my spirit, I don't know; only God knows. But I do know that I was caught up into paradise and heard things so astonishing that they cannot be told."*

"That experience is something worth boasting about, but I am not going to do it. I am going to boast only about my weaknesses. I have plenty to boast about and would be no fool in doing it, because I would be telling the truth. But I won't do it. I don't want anyone to think more highly of me than what they can actually see in my life and my message, even though I have received wonderful revelations from God" (2 Corinthians 12:1–7).

John the Revelator gives this account:

I am John, your brother. In Jesus we are partners in suffering and in the Kingdom and in patient endurance. I was exiled to the Island of Patmos for preaching the word of God and speaking about Jesus. It was the Lord's Day, and I was worshiping in the Spirit. Suddenly, I heard a loud voice behind me, a voice that sounded like a trumpet blast. It said, "[Amen,] write down what you see, and send it to the seven churches: Ephesus, Smyrna, Pergamum, Thyatira, Sardis, Philadelphia, and Laodicea."

When I turned to see who was speaking to me, I saw seven gold lampstands. And standing in the middle of the lampstands was the Son of Man. He was wearing a long robe with a gold sash across his chest. His head and his hair were white like wool, as white as snow. And his eyes were bright like flames of fire. His feet were as bright as bronze refined in a furnace, and his voice thundered like mighty ocean waves. He held seven stars in his right hand, and a sharp two-edged sword came from his mouth. And his face was as bright as the sun in all its brilliance.

When I saw him, I fell at his feet as dead. But he laid his right hand on me and said, "Don't be afraid! I am the First and the Last. I am the living one who died. Look, I am alive forever and ever! And I hold the keys of death and the grave. Write down what you have seen—both the things that are now happening and the things that will happen later" (Revelation 1:9–19).

Yes, JESUS IS ALL WE NEED! Amen!

---

1 "Jesus Is All the World to Me . . .," p. 1, http://library.timelesstruths.org/music/Jesus_Is_All_the_World_to_Me/; Internet; accessed 10 November 2009.

PART 3
LIVING FOREVER IN CHRIST

11

ETERNAL LIFE

Jesus set the stage for us in John 6 when He told the Jews that they should seek the eternal life that He was offering them. By this, He meant that nothing else is as important as our eternity, and nothing should be put ahead of it. And we should be actively seeking it whether we are in poverty or living in the finest luxury. He states it this way in verse 27: *"But you shouldn't be so concerned about perishable things like food. Spend your energy seeking the eternal life that I, the Son of Man, can give you. . . ."*

Eternal life far surpasses anything this world has to offer. What more can people ask for than to live forever and experience the joys of heaven and all the riches such a life offers? In heaven, we will have everything we have ever wanted and everything we will ever need. All our saved love ones will be there; all the saved people we have heard about will be there. The prophets will be there and the apostles will be there. And God will be there. Plus, we will not have sorrow anymore.

Personally, I am looking forward to seeing my father again. I often think about him. He taught me to love God and His Son Jesus. He taught me to love my neighbors. He taught me to love my family, and he taught me to love my country. When I see him, I will be overjoyed. I don't know what I will say to him; maybe I will not say anything. Maybe I will just cry. But they will be tears of joy.

Also, I want to see Steven, the first Christian to be killed for preaching the Gospel. This was shortly after the death of Jesus, right after he preached his first sermon. He chided the Jews for their resistance to Jesus and their opposition to the Holy Spirit. They took him outside Jerusalem and killed him by stoning. I will ask him to tell me what was going through his mind, and how it felt to give his life in the service of God.

Jesus made reference to eternity in Exodus 20:12 when He told the Jews, *"Honor your father and mother. Then you will live a long, full life in the land the Lord your God will give you."*

Yes, Jesus was talking about the land of Canaan. But Canaan was only a type. In the spiritual light, He was talking about heaven. You can't live forever in heaven unless you have eternal life. This is what He means by a *"long, full life."*

Think about it this way. Going to Canaan and living for awhile and then dying is not something I would be too happy about. What good would it do me? I would just leave all my worldly good to someone else. I can do that where I am now. The Christian is promised something much better than Canaan. He is promised a land where he will never grow old, and where he will never get tired from too much hard work. Eternal life does this for us.

The early Christians had heaven in mind when they sold much of their goods and shared the proceeds with those who did not have. It is recorded like this: *"All the believers were of one heart and mind, and they felt that what they owned was not their own; they shared everything they had. And the apostles gave powerful witness to the resurrection of the Lord Jesus, and God's great favor was upon them all"* (Acts 4:32–33).

They knew that when they got to heaven everything would be restored to them and in a much greater way. We have lost sight of this in our theology. As a result, heaven was not in our minds. Instead, many of us are caught up in worldly pleasures and sensual living. We watch any kind of movie. We do any kinds of dances. We visit any kind of place. And we don't even think about what this is doing to our minds. Instead, we just go along as if it is the normal thing to do.

When I am around some Christians, I can't tell them from the world's people. I am forced to ask then what church they attend, or if they go to church. And then, I don't linger long on the subject because it makes them uneasy. If they do talk about church, they only tell me what a great church it is or that if I come, I will have a good time, or that I will be welcome. But they tell me nothing about Jesus and heaven. But the clincher is they never tell me about eternal life. They don't seem to know what it is. If they know anything about it at all, they talk in terms of a social relationship, such as being a friend of God and living with Him. That is part of it, but its greatest asset is that it changes our composition from physical to spirit. It is a conversion to a spirit composition that enables us to escape death.

Then they always get back to the physical and how God will bless me if I attend their church. This amounts to looking down on people. This upsets me because in this world, if you do not have the means to purchase something, it is most difficult for you to get it. As a result, people ignore you and count you as nothing. When you come into their circle, they tend to look away, or otherwise disrespect you. But this is not what God wants for His people. I am not saying that we must do like the first saints did; that was just what God inspired them to do then. But we must not look down on any of God's people. This shows an attitude of humility.

Jesus told us to express this humility by taking the lowest seat at a banquet. Then if the host wants to elevate us, he will. He said this to show us what salvation is like. Namely, God takes us from our low position as sinners and seats us with Him in the highest heavens (Luke 14:10).

Jesus is not against the idea of people being successful in life, far from it. But the trouble is our success tends to take our minds off what is really important. It leads us to look at only the here and now, and not look at where we will spend eternity. It leads us to lavish temporal gifts on our children, instead of teaching them about God. And it leads us to pray only for physical blessings, instead of spiritual blessings.

Let's state it this way. It's all a matter of what or who we look to for salvation. If we look to what this life can offer, we will die. If we look to what Jesus offers, we will live. Jesus is the One who gives us life. Jesus is the One who sustains life. Jesus is the One who feeds and clothes us in this life. Jesus is the One who can take us to the next life. Jesus said if we try to keep our lives in this world, we will lose them altogether.

This equates the lust for the bountiful life to the pleasures sin offers in the world. That is, many people indulge in all types of fun and pleasure without the slightest regard for the future of their souls. They live as if God does not see them, or as if God does not care, or has no plans to judge them for their sins. But in the end, this type of attitude always ends in disaster.

Jesus had a conversation with a rich young man about this same question:

"Someone came to Jesus with this question: 'Teacher, what good things must I do to have eternal life?'

"'Why ask me about what is good?' Jesus replied. 'Only God is good. But to answer your question, you can receive eternal life if you keep the commandments.'

"'Which ones?' the man asked.

"And Jesus replied: 'Do not murder. Do not commit adultery. Do not steal. Do not testify falsely. Honor your father and mother. Love your neighbor as yourself.'

"'I've obeyed all these commandments,' the young man replied. 'What else must I do?'

"Jesus told him, 'If you want to be perfect, go and sell all you have and give the money to the poor, and you will have treasure in heaven. Then come, follow me.' But when the young man heard this, he went sadly away because he had many possessions" (Matthew 19:16–22).

This is a sad commentary on the Jewish nation. By the time of Jesus, they had reduced God's teachings to a ritual of do's and don'ts, that is, a long list of regulations without any spiritual significant. What does it profit how many rules you abide by or how many disciplines you submit to? If you do not have the love of Jesus in you, it is all for nothing. If you do not have the love of Jesus in you, you will not go to heaven.

Yes, Jesus wants us to live forever with Him in heaven. Another way to say it is the sole purpose of Jesus coming to this world was to give His life on the cross so that we who believe in Him can be counted as righteous and be given everything we have ever wanted.

Jesus proved this by what He said about John. *"Who is this man in the wilderness that you went out to see? Did you find him weak as a reed, moved by every breath of wind? Or were you expecting to see a man dressed in expensive clothes? Those who dress like that live in palaces, not out in the wilderness. Were you looking for a prophet? Yes, and he is more than a prophet. John is the man to whom the Scriptures refer when they say, 'Look, I am sending my messenger before you, and he will prepare your way before you'"* (Matthew 11:7–10).

He followed this up by making this emphatic statement in verse 11: *"I assure you, of all who have ever lived, none is greater than John the Baptist. Yet even the most insignificant person in the Kingdom is greater than he is!"* That is, if John was not in the kingdom, he would be considered insignificant. But John was in the kingdom because he was righteous and had eternal life.

Our Christian life, then, should be spent in service to God. This prepares us for what Jesus offers. Jesus wants us to pass from this present state and enter a state that has no death or decay. Wouldn't it be nice not to have aches and pains, worries and fears, or anxious thoughts about what will happen tomorrow? That's the way it will be in heaven. It bothers me, then, that we don't set our sights on heaven, or we don't make mention of it in our prayers. It bothers me, too, that we don't talk about heaven to our children.

We can't stay in this world forever. Jesus said to His listeners:

> *Don't store up treasures here on earth, where they can be eaten by moths and get rusty, and where thieves break in and steal. Store your treasures in heaven, where they will never become moth eaten or rusty and where they will be safe from thieves. Wherever your treasure is, there your heart and thoughts will also be. . . .*
>
> *No one can serve two masters. For you will hate one and love the other, or be devoted to one and despise the other. You cannot serve both God and money.*
>
> *So I tell you, don't worry about everyday life—whether you have enough food, drink, and clothes. Doesn't life consist of more than food and clothing? Look at the birds. They don't need to plant or harvest or put*

> *food in barns because your heavenly Father feeds them. And you are far more valuable to him than they are. Can all your worries add a single moment to your life? Of course . . . [they can't].*
>
> *And why worry about your clothes? Look at the lilies and how they grow. They don't work or make their clothing, yet Solomon in all his glory was not dressed as beautifully as they are. And if God cares so wonderfully for flowers that are here today and gone tomorrow, won't he more surely care for you? You have so little faith!*
>
> *So don't worry about having enough food or drink or clothing. Why be like the pagans who are so deeply concerned about these things? Your heavenly Father already knows all your needs, and he will give you all you need from day to day if you live for him and make the Kingdom of God your primary concern.*
>
> *So don't worry about tomorrow, for tomorrow will bring its own worries. Today's trouble is enough for today* (Matthew 6:19–34).

To put it in plain words, I would rather live forever with Jesus than to have anything else. Think about it this way. Adam was kicked out of the garden into an environment that was hostile to his existence. But he could walk across the field and find gold, silver, diamonds, jewels, oil, any anything else he wanted. And he, through his descendants, has done this. But they still lacked life. Do you see the point?

Without life, the grave is our destiny and hell is our home. This may sound harsh, but it is true. Why can't people see this? Is it too deep and complicated for us to see? Or is it that we don't want to see it? I believe that most people don't want to see it. And what a shame it is!

The prophet Jeremiah endured much hardship to gain eternal life. Jeremiah was turned on by his own brothers (Jeremiah 12:6). The priest Pashur ben Immer, a Temple official, sought out Jeremiah to have him beaten and put in stocks. Hananiah, a false prophet, opposed his preaching. He was mobbed by priests and prophets, and King Jedekiah had him put in jail. He also was accused of being a traitor to his country. Other disciplines (Jeremiah 16:1–13) Jeremiah endured were, not marrying or fathering children, not going to funerals, not sitting in a house where feasting was taking place, or not sitting in the company of merrymakers. Besides this, He was thrown down a well.

Jeremiah 38:1–7 reads:

> *Now Shephatiah son of Mattan, Gedaliah son of Pashhur, Jehucal son of Shelemiah, and Pashhur son of Malkijan heard what Jeremiah had*

been telling the people. He was saying, "[Yes,] this is what the Lord says: 'Everyone who stays in Jerusalem will die from war, famine, or disease, but those who surrender to the Babylonians will live . . ."

So these officials went to the king and said, "Sir, this man must die! That kind of talk will undermine the moral of the few fighting men we have left, as well as that of all the other people, too. This man is a traitor!"

So King Zedekiah agreed. "All right," he said. "Do as you like. I will do nothing to stop you."

So the officials took Jeremiah from his cell and lowered him by ropes into an empty . . . [well] in the prison yard. It belonged to Malkijan, a member of the royal family. There was no water in the . . . [well], but there was a thick layer of mud at the bottom, and Jeremiah sank down into it.

These experiences encouraged Jeremiah to say in despair: *"Yet I curse the day I was born! [Yes,] may the day of my birth not be blessed? I curse the messenger who told my father, 'Good news—you have a son!' Let him be destroyed like the cities of old that the Lord overthrew without mercy. . . . Oh, that I had died in my mother's womb, that her body had been my grave! Why was I ever born? My entire life has been filled with trouble, sorrow, and shame"* (Jeremiah 20:14–18).

The prophet Isaiah had to walk stripped and barefoot for three years (Isaiah 20:1–3). The prophet Ezekiel had to lie on his side for 390 days and eat measured food (Ezekiel 4:1–6).

The prophet Zechariah was the son of Barachiah. In the days of the Babylonian captivity, he prophesied to the Jews in Jerusalem about the will of the God of Israel (Ezra 5:1). He aided Zerubbabel in the rebuilding of the Temple. According to Jesus (Matthew 23:35), he was killed in the Temple of God between the altar and the sanctuary.

The Book of Hebrews tells us: *". . . But others trusted God and were tortured, preferring to die rather than turn from God and be free. They placed their hope in the resurrection to a better life. Some were mocked, and their backs were cut open with whips. Others were chained in dungeons. Some died by stoning, and some were sawed in half; others were killed with the sword. Some went about in skins of sheep and goats, hungry and oppressed and mistreated. They were too good for this world. They wondered over deserts and mountains, hiding in caves and holes in the ground.*

"All of these people we have mentioned received God's approval because of their faith, yet none of them received all that God had promised. For God [in his wisdom] had far better things in mind for us that would also benefit them, for they can't receive the prize at the end of the race until we finish the race" (Hebrews 11:35–40).

My hope in life is to be counted worthy like these people were. Jesus said it this way (Luke 14:26–28): *"If you want to be my follower you must love me more than your father and mother, wife and children, brothers and sisters—yes, more than your own life. Otherwise, you cannot be my disciple. And you cannot be my disciple if you do not carry your cross and follow me. But don't begin until you count the cost. . . ."*

If we choose to center our lives on Jesus, and His way of life, this world would be a better place. We would not have half the problems that we do. But sadly, this is not the way things are, nor will they ever be in this life.

I will conclude this chapter with the words of the gospel song "Just Over in the Glory Land," by James W. Acuff:

> I've a home prepared where the saints abide,
> Just over in the glory land;
> And I long to be by my Savior's side,
> Just over in the glory land.
>
>> Refrain:
>> Just over in the glory land,
>> I'll join the happy angel band,
>> Just over in the glory land;
>> Just over in the glory land,
>> There with the mighty host I'll stand,
>> Just over in the glory land.
>
> I am on my way to those mansions fair,
> Just over in the glory land;
> There to sing God's praise and His glory share,
> Just over in the glory land.
> What a joyful thought that my Lord I'll see,
> Just over in the glory land;
> And with kindred saved, there forever be,
> Just over in the glory land.
> With the blood-washed throng I will shout and sing,
> Just over in the glory land;
> Glad hosannas to Christ, the Lord and King,
> Just over in the glory land.[1]

---

[1] "Just Over in the Glory Land . . .," p. 1, http://library.timelesstruths.org/music/Just_Over_in_the_Glory_Land/; Internet; accessed 4 March 2010.

12

HEAVEN: THE NEW GARDEN OF EDEN

Have you ever wondered why God takes His people to heaven? The answer will surprise you. Let's see how this story unfolds.

When God created man, man was supposed to walk with Jesus and in His light. But sadly, man did not stay in God's light. He sinned by following Satan's lure of freedom and independence from God. This resulted in man being kicked out of the Garden of Eden to live a lonely and desolate life, one filled with misery and desolation.

Much has been written about man's fall. So I will not spend time on it now. All we have to do is look around at this evil world. We see death and destruction everywhere. Hardly anyone is happy. Misery abounds. Problems are everywhere. The environment is being polluted, and we don't know what to do. There are many other problems that are too numerous to mention.

But it always was God's plan to restore man back to Eden and to restore the universe as well: *"Against its will, everything on earth was subjected to God's curse,"* Paul told us in Romans 8:20–23. *"All creation anticipates the day when it will join God's children in glorious freedom from death and decay. For we know that all creation has been groaning as in the pains of childbirth right up to the present time. And even we Christians, although we have the Holy Spirit within us as a foretaste of future glory, also groan to be released from pain and suffering. We, too, wait anxiously for that day when God will give us our full rights as his children; including the new bodies he has promised us."*

Let's continue: *"Look! I am creating new heavens and a new earth—so wonderful that no one will even think about the old ones anymore,"* God tells us in Isaiah 65:17–19. *"Be glad; rejoice forever in my creation! And look! I will create Jerusalem as a place of happiness. Her people will be a source of joy. I will rejoice in Jerusalem and delight in my people. And the sound of weeping and crying will be heard no more."*

The writer John saw this new heaven and new earth in his famous vision on the island of Patmos: *"And the one sitting on the throne said, 'Look, I am making all things new!' And then he said to me, 'Write this down, for what I tell you is trustworthy and true.' And he also said, 'It is finished! I am the Alpha and the Omega—the Beginning and the End. To all who are thirsty I will give the springs of the water of life without charge! All who are victorious will inherit all these blessings, and I will be their God, and they will be my children.*

'But the cowards who turn away from me, and unbelievers, and the corrupt, and murderers, and the immoral, and those who practice witchcraft, and idol worshipers, and all liars—there . . . [end] is in the lake that burns with fire and sulfur. This is the second death'" (Revelation 21:5–8).

This new universe will be far superior to the one we have now. We have always known this, but didn't fully understand how it could be. But we can understand it now. Heaven is a spiritual place and will be the new universe God will make.

Here are three Scriptures that prove God's new universe (new heavens and new earth) will be a spiritual creation.

> 1. *"How we praise God, the Father of our Lord Jesus Christ, who has blessed us with every spiritual blessing in the heavenly realm . . ."* (Ephesians 1:3).
> 2. *". . . But my Kingdom is not of this world"* (John 18:36).
> 3. *"So Christ has now become the High Priest over the good things that have come. He has entered that great, perfect sanctuary in heaven, not made by human hands and not part of this world"* (Hebrews 9:11).

Just imagine: a new universe composed of spirit, and not physical matter. This will be something special, further proof of God's love for us. He is giving us a construction much like the construction of heaven. And it will be real, every bit as real as heaven is real. I can't wait to see it. I think I will just stand and gaze at it for awhile. Or maybe I will just walk around and see how it feels!

Revelation 21:1 (KJV) tells us that on the new earth there will be *"no more sea"*!

Jamieson-Fausset-Brown Bible Commentary opines: ". . . no more sea—The . . . [Sea] is the type of perpetual unrest. Hence our Lord rebukes it as an unruly hostile troubler of his people. It symbolized the political tumults out of which 'the beast' arose, Re 13:1. As the physical corresponds to the spiritual and moral world, so the absence of sea, after the metamorphosis of the earth by fire, answers to the unruffled state of solid peace, which shall then prevail. . . . Then man shall possess inherent powers, which shall make the sea no longer necessary, but an element which would detract from a perfect state."[1]

The "perfect state" could be a direct reference to the existence of spiritual people, as opposed to physical people! These will be God's people, that is, the ones God purposed for Himself all along.

Isaiah 60:21–22 tells us more: *"All your people will be righteous. They will possess their land forever, for I will plant them there with my own hands in order to bring myself glory. The smallest family will multiply into a large clan. The tiniest group will become a mighty nation. I, the Lord, will bring it all to pass at the right time."*

We shouldn't be surprised that the old earth will be no more. Think about it this way: God wants the very best for us. He does not want us looking at anything we once had; He wants us to look at something new. This is the way God is. He is always giving us something new. That is what salvation is all about; it is a new life. If it were like the old life, no one would want it.

The planets, moons, solar systems, stars, galaxies, nebulas, and everything else God made will be new too.

God will make a new Eden for us to live in. This is what Jesus meant when He said that we will live with Him. Or that He was going home to the Father. He stated it this way in John 17: *"I brought glory to you here on earth by doing everything you told me to do. And now, Father, bring me into the glory we shared before the world began."*

He said it this way to Mary in John 20:17: *"Don't cling to me, for I haven't yet ascended to the Father. But go find my brothers and tell them that I am ascending to my Father and your Father, my God and your God."*

The apostle John calls new Eden the Holy City or New Jerusalem. *"[Amen] . . . he took me in spirit to a great, high mountain, and he showed me the [Holy City], Jerusalem, descending out of heaven from God"* (Revelation 21:10). Thus, the new Eden will be much more beautiful and glorious than the one Adam destroyed. In other words, just as the sin of Adam got us kicked out of our "first home," the old Eden, our faith in Jesus is making us ready to move into our "new home," the new Eden.

But people may ask, "How long will it take for this new Eden to be prepared?" We don't know. All we know is that when it does happen, we will be there. And our stay will be glorious. Just think; we will be there in all its splendor, riches, and wonder. We will be there with the saints of old and the holy angels, who constantly sing praises to God. Moreover, we will be there with the twenty-four elders who fall down and worship Jesus.

In Revelation 7:13–17, one of the twenty-four elders asked John, *"Who are these who are clothed in white? Where do they come from?"*

"*Sir, you are the one who knows,*" John replied.

Then, the elder said to John, "*These are the ones coming out of the great tribulation. They washed their robes in the blood of the Lamb and made them white. That is why they are standing in front of the throne of God, serving him day and night in his Temple. And he who sits on the throne will live among them and shelter them. They will never again be hungry or thirsty, and they will be fully protected from the scorching noontime heat. For the Lamb who stands in front of the throne will be their Shepherd. He will lead them to the springs of life-giving water. And God will wipe away all their tears.*"

The writer of the book of Hebrews spoke about this city:

"*All these faithful ones died without receiving what God had promised them, but they saw it all from a distance and welcomed the promises of God. They agreed that they were no more than foreigners and nomads here on earth. And obviously people who talk like that are looking forward to a country they can call their own.*

"*If they had meant the country they came from, they would have found a way to go back. But they were looking for a better place, a heavenly homeland. That is why God is not ashamed to be called their God, for he has promised a heavenly city for them*" (Hebrews 11:13–16).

Earlier the writer tells us in verses 8–10: "*It was by faith that Abraham obeyed when God called him to leave home and go to another land that God would give him as his inheritance. He went without knowing where he was going. And even when he reached the land God promised him, he lived there by faith—for he was like a foreigner living in a tent. And so did Isaac and Jacob, to whom God gave the same promise. Abraham did this because he was confidently looking forward to a city with eternal foundations, a city designed and built by God.*"

John said this about the city: "*And I saw the holy city, [New] . . . Jerusalem, coming down from God out of heaven like a beautiful bride prepared for her husband. I heard a loud shout from the throne, saying, 'Look, the home of God is now among his people! He will live with them, and they will be his people. God himself will be with them. He will remove all their sorrows, and there will be no more death or sorrow or crying or pain. For the old world and its evils are gone forever'*" (Revelation 21:2–4).

Notice very carefully what is being said here. John saw the HEAVENLY CITY, New Jerusalem, the new Eden, "*coming down from God out of heaven like a beautiful bride prepared for her husband.*" And as it descends, since it is of spiritual construction itself, it sits down on the new spiritual earth God has just created. We know it sits on the new earth because we are told earlier that the old earth has already disappeared.

But some may ask: how can the "spiritual" act like the "physical" in its manifestations and actions? In other words, how can the new spiritual earth act and look like the old physical earth? The answer is: it can, and it will!

Let's look at how scientists believe that objects are held together. The Internet article, "What's in a Touch" states:

When two physical surfaces make contact, we say they are "touching" each other. This contact may make it appear that two different surfaces are actually touching, but in fact, *no atoms of any one object can ever touch the atoms of another*. . . .
Here's a simplified explanation of why this is so:

An atom could be described as a positively charged nucleus, surrounded by a cloud of negatively charged electrons. The *nuclear forces* between these two types of objects is so strong that no earthly condition can cause the electrons to merge with the nucleus, even though they are opposite in charge. There is always a space between them.

When two atoms are forced into "contact" . . . a similar type of force, *electromagnetism*, keeps negatively charged electrons from actually making contact with each other.

Push as hard as you want; you cannot make electrons come into contact . . . It's as if you are pushing with similar poles of two very strong bar magnets; you can push one around with the other, but can never force them together. . . .

But wait a minute . . . what about when you cut something!?!! Don't the scissor blades have to touch what they're cutting in order to cut?

No, they don't. . . . They just push against each other with an electromagnetic force. . . ."[2]

Thus, if atoms don't touch, what holds the matter of the universe together? GOD HOLDS THE UNIVERSE TOGETHER BY HIS MIGHTY POWER! (Colossians 1:17). AND GOD WILL HOLD THE SPIRITUAL UNIVERSE TOGETHER!

God is doing this for us. He loves us and wants everything to be right. He wants us to have all the things this present world can't afford. He wants us to be displayed in a far superior way and to be seen as a special creation. Let's rejoice, then, in what God is doing. Let's rejoice, also, in God's care for us. Moreover, let's rejoice in all that we have to look forward to, and always be thankful that God is doing this only for us, HIS BELOVED BRIDE.

Isn't God good?

Many have longed for heaven all their lives. We struggle to make this life as pleasant as possible. We struggle, too, to make things better for our children and to leave them an inheritance. But the new Eden—heaven—will be their inheritance and ours too. As for me, I will tell everyone I can this good news. I can't make anyone believe it, but I will try.

John told us in Revelation 22:1–2, *"And the angel showed me a pure river with the water of life, clear as crystal, flowing from the throne of God and of the Lamb, coursing down the center of the main street. On each side of the river grew a tree of life, bearing twelve crops of fruit, with a fresh crop each month. The leaves were used for medicine to heal the nations."*

Verses 6–7 reads, *"Then the angel said to me, 'These words are trustworthy and true: "The Lord God, who tells his prophets what the future holds, has sent his angel to tell you what will happen soon."'"*

"Look I am coming soon!" Jesus tells us. *"Blessed are those who obey the prophecy written in this scroll"* (Revelation 22:7).

One of my favorite church hymns is "Sweet Beulah Land," written by Squire Parsons:

> I'm kind of homesick for a country
> To which I've never been before.
> No sad goodbyes will there be spoken,
> And time won't matter anymore
> Beulah Land I'm longing for you,
> And someday on thee I'll stand.
> There my home shall be eternal.
> Beulah Land . . . sweet Beulah Land
> I'm looking now across that river
> To where my faith is gonna end in sight.
> There's just a few more days to labor,
> Then I'll take, my heavenly flight
> Beulah Land I'm longing for you,
> And someday on thee I'll stand.
> There my home shall be eternal.
> Beulah Land . . . sweet Beulah Land [3]

Yes, the new HEAVENLY CITY, New Jerusalem, is the new Eden God is preparing for us. Our minds can't imagine it, but it is the transformation of the present heaven into a new and more glorious place. If we put our trust in Jesus, and believe in Him with all our hearts, we will live with Him there.

Before I end this chapter, let me say that God wants us to be saved. And just think; this God is Jesus. Thus, Jesus is not against us. He is not our enemy. An enemy would make things so hard that no one could do them. He might say, "Climb a mountain," or "swim an ocean." One man thought he was supposed to beat himself with whips. Some people try to march or run for Jesus. Some clean up the sides of the roads for Jesus. But He is not asking us to do these things. All He is asking is that we put our trust in Him. This is GOOD NEWS. It is good news because nothing like this has ever been heard before.

Let's keep on loving Him. Let's keep on believing in Him. Let's believe in Him with all our hearts, all our souls, all our minds, and all our strength!

---

1 ". . . Then I saw a new heaven and a new earth, for the . . .," pp. 1–10, http://bible.cc/revelation/21-1.htm; Internet; accessed 6 May 2010.

2 "What's in a Touch . . .," pp. 1–4, http://www.worsleyschool.net/science/files/touch/touch/html; Internet; accessed 10 January 2010.

3 "Sweet Beulah Land," pp. 1–2, http://www.therarelyherd.com/documents/sweetbeulahland.html; Internet; accessed 1 September 2009.

PART 4
CHRIST IS THE WAY!

13

WHY GOD GAVE US THE LAW

This chapter will examine the law's purpose, why God introduced it to us, and how it works today in the lives of God's people. We will do this by relying on God's word, the Bible, to point us in the right direction.

God gave man His law as an act of mercy. He saw man's desperate condition—man's bewilderment over his sins. This prompted God to set His standards down in codified form, pointing out what man was doing wrong. Paul told us: *"We know these laws are good when they are used as God intended. But they were not made for people who do what is right. They are for people who are disobedient and rebellious, who are ungodly, and sinful . . ."* (1 Timothy 1:8–9).

Paul said earlier: *"Well then, am I suggesting that the law of God is evil? Of course not! The law is not sinful, but it was the law that showed me my sin. [For instance,] I would never have known that coveting is wrong if the law had not said, 'Do not [ever] covet.' But sin took advantage of this law and aroused all kinds of forbidden desires within me! If there were no law, sin would not have that power.*

"I felt fine when I did not understand what the law demanded. But when I learned the truth, I realized I had broken the law and was a sinner, doomed to die. So the good law, which was supposed to show me the way of life, instead gave me the death penalty" (Romans 7:7–10).

Paul tells us in Romans 3:19–20, *"Obviously, the law applies to those to whom it was given, for its purpose is to keep people from having excuses and to bring the entire world into judgment before God. For no one can ever be made right in God's sight by doing what the law commands. For the more we know God's law, the clearer it becomes that we aren't obeying it."* Another way of saying this is when we stand before God on Judgment Day, we will not be able to say to God that we didn't know that what we did was wrong. The law prevents this from happening.

It could be stated this way: by the time Adam was kicked out of the garden, his mind was already locked into a sinful mode. It remained that way for the rest of his life, bringing sin and death to himself and all his children. By default, then, the rest of humanity was in this condition.

This agrees perfectly with what 2 Timothy 3:6–9 tells us about many of our preachers: *"They are the kind who work their way into people's homes and win the confidence of vulnerable women who are burdened with the guilt of sin and controlled by many desires. Such women are forever following new teachings, but they never understand the truth. And these teachers fight the truth just as Jannes and Jambres fought against Moses.*

"Their minds are depraved, and their faith is counterfeit. But they won't get away with this for long. Someday everyone will recognize what fools they are, just as happened with Jannes and Jambres."

We can conclude, therefore, that we have all broken God's laws, no matter how good we think we are. It makes no difference what race we belong to, whether we are rich or poor, male or female, how positive we think, or whatever else we can think of. We have all sinned against God and are in need of God's mercy. So what of the law?

It is still part of the Bible, but its administration over God's people has ended. *"When God speaks of a . . . [New Covenant],"* the writer of Hebrews tells us in Hebrews 8:13, *"it means he has made the first one obsolete. It is now out of date and ready to be put aside."* Those under the New Covenant are saved by God's grace, through faith.

However, I want to make it clear at this point: The Holy Spirit overseas this whole operation. That is, without the Spirit's promptings, no one can understand the law's purpose and demands. In addition, without the Spirit's promptings, no one can come to Jesus to be saved.

We can sum it us this way: the law tells us that it is wrong to have evil thoughts. But if Christ had not come to save us, the law would simply do its job and demand our deaths!

But Christ has come! The Christmas song, "O Come, All Ye Faithful," expresses our adoration for this great event:

> O Come All Ye Faithful
> Joyful and triumphant,
> O come ye, O come ye to Bethlehem.
> Come and behold Him,
> Born the King of Angels;
> O come, let us adore Him,
> O come, let us adore Him,
> O come, let us adore, Him,
> Christ the Lord.

O Sing, choirs of angels,
Sing in exultation,
Sing all that hear in heaven God's holy word.
Give to our Gather glory in the Highest;
O come, let us adore Him,
O come, let us adore Him,
O come, let us adore Him,
Christ the Lord.
All Hail! Lord, we greet Thee,
Born this happy morning,
O Jesus! . . . [For] evermore be Thy name adored.
Word of the Father, now in flesh appearing;
O come, let us adore Him,
O come, let us adore Him,
O come, let us adore Him,
Christ the Lord.[1]

This is a hard concept for most people to understand because we are too steeped in pride and self-righteousness to allow our minds to think along these lines. We want to think that we are good, and that we can save ourselves, or that we don't need any saving at all.

But the law demands our death (Ezekiel 18:20): *"The one who sins is the one who dies . . ."* Thus, God sent Jesus to die in our place. He came to the earth and took our punishment by dying a criminal's death on the cross.

Just think of it: All because of the law's demand, nearly two thousand years ago, a poor, helpless man in His early 30s was executed by crucifixion like a common criminal. He never wrote a book, never pastored a megachurch, never traveled on an airplane, and was never awarded man-of-the-year. Furthermore, He never took a wife, and never had the pleasure of eating a meal in a fine restaurant. Yet, His death saved us all.

Why? Because His death was a substitutional atonement; that is, the law recognized it as a legal replacement for all mankind, and at the same time, the only means by which man could be reconciled to God. That's why the cross is the symbol of the Christian faith and the crux of human history.

Below are three Scriptures proving this point:

- *"As for me, God forbid that I should boast about anything except the cross of our Lord Jesus Christ . . ."* (Galatians 6:14).
- *"I know very well how foolish the message of the cross sounds to those who are on the road to destruction. But we who are being saved recognize this message as the very power of God"* (1 Corinthians 1:18).
- *"For I have told you often before, and I say it again with tears in my*

eyes, that there are many whose conduct shows they are really enemies of the cross of Christ. Their future is eternal destruction. Their god is their appetite . . . and all they think about is this life here on earth" (Philippians 3:18–19).

The first two verses and refrain of the old hymn, "At the Cross," express this view:

> Alas, and did my Savior bleed
> And did my Sov'reign die?
> Would He devote . . . [such a] sacred head
> For such a worm . . . [am] I?
> Was it for crimes that I had done?
> He groaned upon the tree
> Amazing pity! Grace unknown!
> And love beyond degree!
> At the cross, at the cross where I first saw the light
> And the burden of my heart rolled away,
> It was there by faith I received my sight,
> And now I am happy all the day!
> (Written by Isaac Watts, 1707)[2]

Let's make this plain then: trying to keep the law after you have already broken it is useless. The penalty phase of the law is now in effect, and you must be punished. This brings about the necessity of the cross; it places itself in your place.

But if the law had not been given to us, we would not know anything about the righteousness of God or the consequences of our sins. We would spend all of our time believing that we are good and have done nothing wrong. Then, when we heard the Gospel message of repentance and turning to Christ for salvation, we would not see any sins that we needed to repent of or turn from. In other words, if the law had not been given to us, then it could not serve its purpose of pointing out our sins. Then the Holy Spirit could not turn us to Christ for salvation.

Psalm 19:9–11 says the same thing: *". . . The laws of the LORD are true: each one is fair. They are more desirable than gold, even the finest gold. . . . They are a warning to those who hear them. . . ."* Verses 12–13 go on to say: *"How can I know all the sins lurking in my heart? Cleanse me from these hidden faults. . . . Don't let them control me. Then I will be free of guilt and innocent of great sin."*

Let's summarize: the law, itself, can't save us. Its job is to tell us what we have done wrong by showing us our sins. Then the Holy Spirit convicts us of our sins and points us to Christ, who saves us. In other words, the law is only a shadow of the real thing, Christ Himself (Colossians 3:17). Thus at Christ's death (the cross) the administration of the law over our lives ended!

The end of the law's administration is brought out by what we read in Luke 9:28–31: *"About eight days later Jesus took Peter, James, and John to a mountain to pray. And as he was praying, the appearance of his face changed, and his clothing became dazzling white. Then two men, Moses and Elijah, appeared and began talking with Jesus. They were glorious to see. And they were speaking of how he was about to fulfill God's plan by dying in Jerusalem."*

The fact that it was Moses (the one God used to give the law) and Elijah (the one God used to restore the law) is significant because it pictures the fulfilling of what God had these men do and after this, the ushering in of something entirely new. This was accomplished by the death, burial, and resurrection of Christ. This is born out by what God said to the disciples in verse 35: *"This is my Son, my Chosen One. Listen to him."*

But the question still may be asked: the Old Covenant has a lot of good things in it—it tells us how to live. What about this?

The problem was not with the Old Covenant and its laws; the problem was in our inability to keep these laws because of our sinful nature. Something had to be done on God's part; otherwise, no one would ever be saved. God had to provide a new and different way for us to attain perfection. He did this through the forgiveness of sins under the New Covenant.

But let's answer this question: if the Ten Commandments are no longer in effect, wouldn't that make it all right to lie, steal, murder, etc.? The answer is NO! These things are still against God's standards, as pointed out in the New Testament. The reason the Old Covenant is not needed is that Jesus replaced it with a new and better covenant, one demonstrating God's grace and love for us—the Gospel. The New Covenant is also a covenant under which we can live in God's holiness, instead of the fear of punishment.

It is good to point out that Jesus used the word "until" (Matthew 5:18) in reference to the law: *"I assure you [all], until heaven and earth disappear, even the smallest detail of God's law will remain until its purpose is achieved."* This means that the law, and all its binding statutes, be set aside when "all is fulfilled." And all sincere believers know that Jesus made sure that "all was fulfilled."

Luke 16:16 reads, *"Until John the Baptist began to preach, the . . . [Law] of Moses and the message of the prophets were your guides. But now the Good News [the Gospel] of the Kingdom is preached. . . ."* Many other New Testament Scriptures make similar statements.

But let's answer this one last question: if the administration of the law is ended, then why is the Old Testament still part of the Bible? The Old Testament is the foundation for the New Testament. That is, it must be part of the Bible; otherwise, we would see no need for Christ to come and set up the New Covenant.

Glory and honor to the all-wise God!

---

1 "O Come, All Ye Faithful lyrics," <http://www.carols.org.uk/o_come_all_ye_faithful.htm>.;Internet; accessed 1 January 2010, pp. 1–2.

2 "At the Cross . . . Isaac Watt," <http://library.timelesstruths.org/music/At_the_Cross_Hudson/>.; Internet; accessed 6 January 2010, p. 1.

14

THE BIBLICAL MEANING OF TITHING

As a child, I learned about the ritual of tithing very early. But it seemed to me just another way for the church to raise money. Of its spiritual implications, I knew nothing about. I was to learn this much later.

The first indication we see of this is after Abraham gave a tithe in Genesis14. But let's get to the point: This tithe, or tenth, is a picture of Jesus giving Himself to God for our sins. It can be no other way. If Jesus does not do this, then Abraham and all the other prophets, along with us, are doomed to destruction. We will all end up in the lake of fire.

Jesus dying to save is what the Bible is all about. We see this pictured in the life of Abraham. He was in Ur of the Chaldeans, and God brought him out. He lost his wife to the Egyptian king, and God rescued her. Abraham had no natural son; God rescued him by giving him one. The same can be seen in the lives of Isaac and Jacob, as well.

The same is true for the nation of Israel. Isaiah 59:15–20 says, *"The* LORD *looked and was displeased to find that there was no justice. He was amazed to see that no one intervened to help the oppressed. So he himself stepped in to save them with his mighty power and justice. . . . He clothed himself with the robes of vengeance and godly fury. He will repay his enemies for their evil deeds. . . . Then at last they will respect and glorify the name of the* LORD *throughout the world. . . . 'The Redeemer will come to Jerusalem,' says the* LORD, *'to buy back those in Israel who have turned from their sins.'"*

God does not need our money to save us. There was no money displayed at the cross. He introduced it here only to set up a type. He divides the dollar into two parts, 1/10 and 9/10. And as Abraham gave his 1/10 to buy back Lot, so the Father gave His 1/10 to buy back the world, the 9/10.

If you have never thought about tithing this way, don't be saddened.

This picture has been in the Bible all along. We just did not see it. But we see it now. We must teach it to God's people. God wants His people to know that the Old Testament tithing law is more than just giving to the church. It pictures our Lord Jesus, giving Himself for the sins of the world.

In the redemption ceremony of Leviticus 27, we see again the *tenth* as a picture of Christ. A tenth of all the produce of the land, whether grain or fruit, belonged to the Lord and was to be set aside for His holy use. However, if the people wanted to buy back the tenth itself, it could be bought back by paying its value plus 20 percent (Leviticus 27:30–34). This amounted to three tithes—the first tithe plus two additional tithes. This means that the Father and the Holy Spirit played a part in our redemption as well.

People pay tithes to the church because they believe it is commanded by God. But I must ask, didn't God give us many other commands too? For instance, God told us in Leviticus 19:32 to show our respect for God by standing up in the presence of the elderly. But do we do this? He also told us to put to death those who commit adultery in our midst (Leviticus 20:10). Our churches are full of people who commit adultery.

The New Testament is concerned with our salvation. Jesus verified this when He told His followers in Matthew 13:22–23, *"The thorny ground represents those who hear and accept the Good News, but all too quickly the message is crowded out by the cares of this life and the lure of wealth, so no crop is produced. The good soil represents the hearts of those who truly accept God's message and produce a huge harvest—thirty, sixty, or even a hundred times as much as had been planted."*

Paul told Timothy (1 Timothy 6:6–10), *"Yet true religion with contentment is great wealth. After all, we didn't bring anything with us when we came into the world, and we certainly cannot carry anything with us when we die. So if we have enough food and clothing, let us be content. But people who long to be rich fall into temptation and are trapped by many foolish and harmful desires that plunge them into ruin and destruction. For the love of money is at the root of all kinds of evil. And some people, craving money, have wandered from the faith and pierced themselves with many sorrows."*

King David didn't rejoice in his wealth. He rejoiced in his salvation!

"The king shall joy in thy strength, O LORD; and in thy salvation how greatly shall he rejoice! Thou hast given him his heart's desire, and hast not witholden the request of his lips. For thou preventest him with the blessings of goodness: thou settest a crown of pure gold on his head. He asked life of thee, and thou gavest it him, even length of days . . . [forever] and ever. His glory is great in thy salvation: honor and majesty hast thou . . . [lain] upon him. For thou hast made him most blessed for ever: thou hast made him exceeding glad with thy countenance. For the king trustesth in the LORD, and through the mercy of the most High he shall not be moved" (Psalm 21:1–7, KJV).

Solomon made this statement on the subject:

Vanity of vanities, saith the Preacher, vanity of vanities; all is vanity. What profit hath a man of all his labor which he taketh under the sun? One generation passeth away, and another generation cometh: but the earth abideth . . . [forever]. The sun also ariseth, and the sun goeth down, and hasteth to his place where he arose. . . .

All things are full of labour; man cannot utter it: the eye is not satisfied with seeing, nor the ear filled with hearing. . . . There is no remembrance of former things; neither shall there be any remembrance of things that are to come with those that shall come after. . . .

I have seen all the works that are done under the sun; and, behold, all is vanity and vexation of spirit (Ecclesiastes 1:2–11, KJV).

Near the end of this discourse, Solomon concluded:

Remember now thy Creator in the days of thy youth, while the evil days come not, nor the years draw nigh, when thou shalt say, I have no pleasure in them; While the sun, or the light, or the moon, or the stars, be not darkened, nor the clouds return after the rain. . . . Or ever the silver cord be loosed, or the golden bowl be broken, or the pitcher be broken at the fountain, or the wheel broken at the cistern.

Then shall the dust return to the earth as it was: and the spirit shall return unto God who gave it.

Vanity of vanities, saith the preacher; all is vanity. . . .

Let us hear the conclusion of the whole matter: Fear God, and keep his commandments: for this is the whole duty of man. For God shall bring every work into judgment, with every secret thing . . . (Ecclesiastes 12, KJV).

Paul faced the same dilemma during his ministry. He was beset with a problem that tormented him to no end. Some say it was poor eyesight, others think it might have been some other physical problem. But in any case, it placed severe limitations upon him. At first, he wanted God to take it away. But later he concluded that God knew what was best for him, and that God would see him through every trial, no matter how difficult it was. He also concluded that oftentimes God works best through us when we appear weak to the world.

"Three different times I begged the Lord to take it away," Paul tells us. *"Each time he said, 'My gracious favor is all you need. My power works best in your weakness.' So now I am glad to boast about my weaknesses, so that the power of Christ may work*

through me. Since I know it is all for Christ's good, I am quite content with my weaknesses and with insults, hardships, persecutions, and calamities. For when I am weak, then I am strong" (2 Corinthians 12:8–10).

During his ministry, one of Paul's biggest concerns was the collection of money for the poor saints at Jerusalem. He told the believers in Corinth, *"On every Lord's Day, each of you should put aside some amount of money in relation to what you have earned and save it for this offering. . . . When I come I will write letters of recommendation for the messengers you choose to deliver your gift to Jerusalem"* (1 Corinthians 16:2–3).

John the Baptist lived out in the desert most of his adult life. His food was wild honey and locusts. He made his own clothing. He had no toothbrush, automobile, savings account, house to live in, or any of the modern appliances we now depend on. Yet, Jesus said that no man ever born was greater than John.

When we accept Jesus as our Savior, the Holy Spirit comes to live in us, gives us eternal life (John 6:63), and makes us able to do the good works God wants us to do. Then at Christ's return, He will take us home to live with Him in heaven where we will never want for anything again (Revelation 21:4, 22:3). What better blessings can we have than this?

"Can we boast, then, that we have done anything to be accepted by God? No, because our acquittal is not based on our good deeds. It is based on our faith. So we are made right with God through faith and not by obeying the law," Paul said in Romans 3:27–30. *"After all, God is not the God of the Jews only, is he? Isn't he also the God of the Gentiles? Of course he is. There is only one God, and there is only one way of being accepted by him. He makes people right with himself only by faith. . . ."*

The faith we are talking about is faith in His death!

By dying for us, Jesus freed us from the guilt of our sins and restored us to God by providing the needed payment God required for our sins. His blood paid our sin debt, forever, making us friends of God. God can now show mercy to us because Christ has satisfied the claims of justice. It is not often that an advocate (or lawyer) pays for his client's sins; yet that is what our Lord has done, and most remarkable of all, He paid for them by the sacrifice of Himself.

Our salvation is worth more than all the riches in the world. All those who received physical blessings under the Old Covenant died, just like the people around them. But those who are blessed with salvation through Christ will live forever. *"Many of those whose bodies lie dead and buried will rise up, some to everlasting life and some to shame and everlasting contempt,"* Daniel said in Daniel 12:2.

The prophet Isaiah prophesied: *"LORD, in distress we searched for you. We were bowed beneath the burden of your discipline. . . . Yet we have this assurance: Those who belong to God will live; their bodies will rise again! Those who sleep in the earth will rise up and sing for joy! For God's light of life will fall like dew on his people in the place of the dead!"* (Isaiah 26:16–19).

Jesus, in John 17:1–21, applied this prophecy to Himself as the One who makes it happen: *"Father, the time has come. Glorify your Son so he can give glory back to you. [Yes,] . . . you have given him authority over everyone in all the earth. He gives eternal life to each one you have given him. . . . I am praying not only for these disciples but also for all who will ever believe in me because of their testimony. My prayer for all of them is that they will be one, just as you and I are one, Father—that just as you are in . . . [I] and I . . . in you, so they will be in us, and the world will believe you sent me."*

Now here is the point I want to make: Jesus' death fulfilled all the requirements of the law, including the tithing law: *"You have died with Christ, and he has set you free from the evil powers of this world,"* Paul told us. *"So why do you keep on following rules of this world, such as 'Don't handle, don't eat, don't touch.' Such rules are mere human teachings about things that are gone as soon as you use them. These rules may seem wise because they require strong devotion, humility, and severe bodily discipline. But they have no effect when it comes to conquering a person's evil thoughts and desires"* (Colossians 2:20–23).

Earlier Paul had said this to the Colossian Christians:

> *Don't let anyone lead you astray with empty philosophy and high-sounding nonsense that come from human thinking and from the evil powers of this world, and not from Christ. For in Christ the fullness of God lives in a human body, and you are complete through your union with Christ. He is the Lord over every ruler and authority in the universe.*
>
> *You were dead because of your sins and because . . . [the] sinful nature was not yet cut away. Then God made you alive with Christ. He forgave all our sins. He canceled the record [the law] that contained the charges against us. He took it and destroyed it by nailing it to Christ's cross. In this way, God disarmed the evil rulers and authorities. He shamed them publicly by his victory over them on the cross of Christ"* (Colossians 2:8–10, 13–15).

The writer of Hebrews sums it up this way in Hebrews 9:14–15: *"Just think how much more the blood of Christ will purify our hearts from deeds that lead to death so that we can worship the living God. For by the power of the eternal Spirit, Christ offered himself to God as a perfect sacrifice for our sins. That is why he is the one who mediates the . . . [New Covenant] between God and . . . people . . . that all who are invited can receive the eternal inheritance God has promised them. For Christ died to set them free from the penalty of the sins they had committed under the first covenant."*

Paul tells us that each of us is responsible to the Lord on a personal basis. He also tells us that God's power will help us to know how much to give, and in what way we must use our giving to please Him. Thus, whether we give 1 percent, 10 percent, or some other amount, we should always be careful to follow the advice that Paul has given to us. Then we will be doing the will of God, and giving to Him because we truly love Him, and not because we are forced to by the law.

Paul told the Corinthian believers in 2 Corinthians 8:10–13, *"I suggest that you finish what you started a year ago, for you were the first to propose this idea, and you were the first to begin doing something about it. Now you should carry this project through to completion just as enthusiastically as you began it. Give whatever you can . . . [in accords] to what you have. If you are really eager to give, it isn't important how much you are able to give. God wants you to give what you have, not what you don't have. Of course, I don't mean you should give so much that you suffer from having too little. I only mean that there should be some equality."*

He added in 2 Corinthians 9:7–8: *"You must each make up your own mind as to how much you should give. Don't give reluctantly or in response to pressure. . . . God loves the person who gives cheerfully. And God will generously provide all you need. . . ."*

God bless you!

15

WHO IS THE BEAST?

The adversary of God has always been Satan. Satan first set himself up against God in heaven when his pride forced him into rebellion, resulting in his ouster. Now he is on earth, and his rebellion continues. He is God's enemy, an as a result, he is referred to in the Bible as the beast.

"And now in my vision I saw a beast rising up out of the sea. It had seven heads and ten horns, with ten crowns on its horns. And written on each head were names that blasphemed God," John told us in Revelation 13:1–4. *"This beast looked like a leopard, but it had bear's feet and a lion's mouth! And the dragon gave him his own power and throne and great authority.*

"I saw that one of the heads of the beast seemed wounded beyond recovery—but the fatal wound was healed! All [of the people of] the world marveled at this miracle and followed the beast in awe. They worshiped the dragon for giving the beast such power, and they worshiped the beast. 'Is there anyone as great as the beast?' they exclaimed. 'Who is able to fight against him?'" (Revelation 13:1–4).

This beast is described as a leopard, a bear, and a lion, all combined into one, testifying to its power to destroy or rule over people. The mention of its death and recovery is a reference to Satan's defeat by Christ at the cross, and his subsequent resurgence to torment of God's people. But as he is doing this, he performs miracles, deceiving the people into false worship.

That Satan is our enemy there is no doubt: *"A final word: Be strong with the Lord's mighty power. Put on all of God's armor so that you will be able to stand firm against all strategies and tricks of the Devil,"* Paul told us in Ephesians 6:10–12. *". . . For we are not fighting against people made of flesh and blood, but against the evil rulers and authorities of the unseen world, against those mighty powers of darkness who rule this world, and against wicked spirits in heavenly realms."*

1 Thessalonians 2:17–19 tells us this: *"Dear brothers and sisters, after we were separated from you for a little while (though our hearts never left you), we tried very hard to come back because of our intense longing to see you again. We wanted very much to come, and I, Paul, tried again and again, but Satan prevented us. After all, what gives us hope and joy, and what is our proud reward and crown? It is you! Yes, you will bring us much joy as we stand together before our Lord Jesus when he comes back again."*

We must see Satan, then, as God intends for us to see him; otherwise, we won't understand the Scriptures. He fights against God every chance he gets. As Paul warned us to do, we must fight against him with all our might (2 Corinthians 10:3–6). If we do not fight against him, he will consume us as surely as a lion or some other wild animal consumes a helpless animal in the field.

Peter said he fills our hearts with evil (Acts 5:3). John 13:2 says that Satan entices us to betray Jesus. In 2 Corinthians 2:11, it says that Satan tries to outsmart us. Revelation 12:4 says that He drew one-third of the angels to earth with him.

The book of Revelation tells us: *"Then the beast [Satan] was allowed to speak great blasphemies against God. And he was given authority to do what he wanted to for forty-two months. And he spoke terrible words of blasphemy against God, slandering his name and all who live in heaven; who are his temple. And the beast was allowed to wage war against God's holy people and to overcome them. And he was given authority to rule over every tribe and people and language and nation.*

"And all the people who belong to this world worshiped the beast . . ." (Revelation 13:5–8).

That Satan blasphemes God there is no doubt either. But much of the time, this blasphemy is subtle. What I mean is, he doesn't make outrights attacks. This would be noticed by everyone, and it wouldn't work. His attack is more like what he used against Eve in the garden. He cast doubt on God's word, causing her to sin. This made him God in her eyes.

This same strategy is used today. I hear so many sermons changing the meaning and intent of the words of Jesus. Then the preacher leads the people to do the opposite of what Jesus would have us do. The people don't seem to know any better, or they don't seem to notice the difference. All it takes is to change the meaning of one word of a Scripture, and you can distort its entire meaning.

But unbeknown to most people, Satan employs a host of demons as his assistants. Their exact number is unknown, but it is considerable. They are invisible to us, but you can see their presence in the personalities of people around you. What else can people expect, after giving themselves over completely to the adoration and worship of Satan? They desired to have Satan rule over them, and now God is allowing it to happen. These demons torment and frustrate them right up until their last day on earth.

Consider this personal testimony of an unnamed preacher:

That demons can cause harm to people there is no doubt! Their actions are not often understood or noticed by the casual observer because demons are selective in their targeting. That is, they do not target everyone in a group; they only attack certain people. You may see it happening to people and never understand what is taking place. They also often attack in the name of God, or under a religious pretense. They do this by claiming that they are doing God's will, or that the victim deserves what is happening to them.

Some demons congregate—they attack in mass, usually led by a super-demon, who commands the others.

By *congregate*, I mean that they group themselves in selected areas, intending to hurt selected people. We know this is so by what we read in Scriptures such as Joel 2:2 and Revelation 9:1–11.

But demons are most effective when they enter the personalities of people. Demons were in the personality of the man in the synagogue in Capernaum:

. . . A man possessed by an evil spirit was in the synagogue, and he began shouting, "Why are you bothering us, Jesus of Nazareth? Have you come to destroy us? I know who you are—the Holy One sent from God!"

Jesus cut him short. "Be silent! Come out of the man." At that, the evil spirit screamed and threw the man into a convulsion, but then he left him.

Amazement gripped the audience, and they began to discuss what had happened. "What sort of new teaching is this?" they asked excitedly. "It has such authority! Even the evil spirits obey his orders!" (Mark 1:23–27).

When Jesus arrived at the other side of the lake, He met a man possessed by many demons. Jesus asked the man his name. "Legion," the man replied. By *legion* the man meant that he was possessed by thousands of demons.

Another example is seen in what took place after Jesus came down from the Mountain of Transfiguration:

At the foot of the mountain they found a great crowd surrounding the other disciples. . . . The crowd watched Jesus in awe as he came toward them, and then they ran to greet him. "What is all this arguing about?" he asked.

One of the men in the crowd spoke up and said, "Teacher, I brought my son for you to heal him. He can't speak because he is possessed by an evil spirit that won't let him talk. And whenever this evil spirit seizes him, it throws him violently to the ground and makes him foam at the mouth and grind his teeth and become rigid. So I asked your disciples to cast out the evil spirit, but they couldn't do it."

Jesus said to them, "You faithless people! How long must I be with you until you believe? How long must I put up with you? Bring the boy to me." So they brought the boy. But when the evil spirit saw Jesus, it threw the child into a violent convulsion, and he fell to the ground, writhing and foaming at the mouth. "How long has this been happening?" Jesus asked the boy's father.

He replied, "Since he was very small. The evil spirit often makes him fall into the fire or into water, trying to kill him. Have mercy on us and help us. Do something if you can." "What do you mean . . ." Jesus asked. "Anything is possible if a person believes."

The father instantly replied, "I do believe, but help me not to doubt!" When Jesus saw that the crowd of onlookers was growing, he rebuked the evil spirit. "Spirit of deafness and muteness," he said, "I command you to come out of this child and never enter him again!" Then the spirit screamed and threw the boy into another violent convulsion and left him. The boy lay there motionless, and he appeared to be dead. A murmur ran through the crowd, "He's dead." But Jesus took him by the hand and helped him to his feet, and he stood up (Mark 9:14–27).

Under demonic influence, a "preacher's wife" provoked an entire classroom of students to attack me. She personally called each of the student's parents, encouraging them to incite their children to disobey my authority. Then she incited the school authorities to attack me because I could not stop the students from rebelling. This is how Satan works. He creates a mess, and then he condemns God's people for allowing the mess to happen.

I knew they were demons by the tactics they used. God is love. God does not incite harm upon people. God does not use foul or abusive language. God does not violate His own laws, i.e., disrespect authority, tell lies, steal, make mischief, create chaos, deliberately displace items, start fights, mislead authority, etc., all in the name of being a good person.

I never saw their form or shape, but I knew they were there.

I sensed their presence!

Thankfully, God protected me by removing me from the situation.

The preacher's wife continued with her religious work, never realizing that she was under demonic control.

Before we were saved, we all were under Satan's control:

"Once you were dead, [and] doomed forever because of your many sins. You used to live just like the rest of the world, full of sin, obeying Satan, the mighty prince of the power of the air. He is the spirit at work in the hearts of those who refuse to obey God.

"All of us used to live that way, following the passions and desires of our evil nature. We were born with an evil nature, and we were under God's anger just like everyone else" (Ephesians 2:1–3).

To combat demons, we must pray to Jesus for protection. When I was a child, I often heard people praying this way. They would say, "Jesus save me, Jesus protect me!" "Jesus I need you!" Some people would just say, "Lord have mercy; help me, Lord." For those who refused to pray to Jesus, the torment seemed to continue.

We can just bow our heads and say, "I am in trouble, here, Lord. These demons are attacking me, and I don't know what to do. I can't stop them." And if Jesus desires it so, the attacks will stop.

But sometimes Jesus allows the attacks to continue for some time. I am not sure of the exact reason, but it may be He wants to test us to see if we will remain faithful to Him. Or it may be for some other reason. But in all cases, Jesus knows what is best for us.

Jesus said this to Moses: *"I am the God of your ancestors—the God of Abraham, the God of Isaac, and the God of Jacob. You can be sure I have seen the misery of my people in Egypt. I have heard their cries for deliverance from their harsh slave drivers. Yes, I am aware of their suffering"* (Exodus 3:7).

Here, slavery in Egypt is a type of the suffering God's people undergo from demons. This means that Jesus is always aware of our problems, and is concerned for us. Call to Him then, and let His will be done in your life.

David said in Psalm 42:13–16: *"The LORD will march forth like a mighty man; he will come out like a warrior, full of fury. He will shout his thundering battle cry, and he will crush all his enemies. He will say, 'I have long been silent; yes, I have restrained myself. But now I will give full vent to my fury; I will gasp and pant . . . [as] a woman giving birth.*

"'I will level the mountains and hills and bring . . . blight on all their greenery. I will turn the rivers into dry land and will dry up all the pools. I will lead Israel down a new path, guiding them along an unfamiliar way. I will make the darkness bright before

them and smooth out the road ahead of them. Yes, I will indeed do these things; I will not forsake them.'"

It is so sad that so many of God's people don't look at Jesus this way. It was once widely taught in the Christian circles, but now it is being discarded as being old fashioned and out of date. Hopefully, the writing of this book will change this.

The words of the beloved hymn "Faith of Our Fathers" tell the story best:

> Faith of our fathers, living still,
> In spite of dungeon, fire, and sword;
> Oh, how our hearts beat high with joy
> Whene'er we hear that glorious Word!
> Refrain:
> Faith of our fathers, holy faith!
> We will be true . . . [indeed] till death
> Faith of our fathers, we will strive
> To sin all nations unto thee;
> And through the truth that comes from God,
> We all shall then be truly free.
> Faith of our fathers, we will love
> Both friends and foe in all our strife;
> And preach thee, too, as love knows how
> By kindly words and virtuous life![1]

But most important of all, we must become saved!

Without salvation, no one has protection from Satan. This means that we must always be about His work. Jesus said it this way in Matthew 9:37–38: *"The harvest is so great, but the workers are so few. So pray to the Lord who is in charge of the harvest; ask him to send out more workers for his fields."*

He said the same thing in Matthew 22:18–21: *"'You hypocrites! Whom are you trying to fool with your trick questions? Here, show me the Roman coin used for the tax. Whose picture and title are stamped on it?'*

"The people answered, 'Caesar's.'

"'Well then,' Jesus remarked. 'Give to Caesar what belongs to him. But everything that belongs to God must be given to God.'"

God bless us!

---

[1] "Faith of Our Fathers . . .," <http://library.timelesstruths.org/music/Faith_of_Our_Fathers/>.;Internet; accessed 12 April 2010, p. 1.

16

SATAN: THE ABOMINATION OF DESOLATION

In the previous chapter, we saw that Satan is called the beast. But why is he also called the abomination of desolation? Clearly, this is a warning to all who are wise enough to take note.

Jesus said it this way: *"When ye therefore shall see the ABOMINATION OF DESOLATION, spoken of by Daniel the prophet, stand in the holy place, (whoso readeth, let him understand:) Then let them which be in Judae'-a flee into the mountains: Let him which is on the housetop not come down to take any thing out of his house: Neither let him which is in the field return back to take his clothes. And woe unto them that are with child, and to them that give suck in those days! But pray ye that your flight be not in the winter, neither on the sabbath day"* (Matthew 24:15–20, KJV).

This means that if you are on an important assignment for Jesus, do not let Satan, or anyone else stop you. This must be true even if your personal property, personal safety, or health is threatened. This is especially true if the threat comes from religious circles. God's work is more important.

But Satan will try to stop God's work!

Isaiah 14:12–15 says this about Satan: *"How you are fallen from heaven, O shining star, son of the morning! You have been thrown down to the earth, you who destroyed the nations of the world. For you said to yourself, 'I will ascend to heaven and set my throne above God's stars. I will preside on the mountain of the gods far away in the north. I will climb to the highest heavens and be like the Most High.' But instead, you will be brought down to the place of the dead, down to its lowest depths.*

"Everyone there will stare at you and ask, 'Can this be the one who shook the earth and the kingdoms of the world? Is this the one who destroyed the world and made it into a wilderness? Is this the king who demolished the world's greatest cities and had no mercy on his prisoners?'"

This must be pointed out without delay. Satan wants very much to be God. In this effort, he often mimics God's actions. This is why we see miracles among his people too. And these miracles are real. They are not pretend. People testify at great lengths about how they were healed or cured of a disease. And we know these people are in a false church. Sometimes these churches are openly hostile to true religion.

But remember that Satan has another side he displays too. He often destroys and tears down that which he comes into contact with. Sometimes this is after propping it up to make it appear as something blessed of God. Or propping it up to make it appear as something people should desire. But destroy he does. We wonder why great civilizations fall without any explanation. The above verses say that Satan is the reason.

Ezekiel 28:15–17 comments: *"You were blameless in all you did from the day you were created until the day evil was found in you. Your great wealth filled you with violence, and you sinned. So I banished you from the mountain of God. I expelled you, O mighty guardian, from your place among the stones of fire. Your heart was filled with pride because of all your beauty. You corrupted your wisdom for the sake of your splendor. So I threw you to the earth and exposed you to the curious gaze of kings."*

This is a warning to all God's people. Satan is here, and he is actively at work. We must be on guard at all times, constantly watching for any sign of his presence. The way to do this is to look at the actions of the people around you. We can look at our circumstances, as well. Satan's influence is usually opposite of the influence God would display. God is a God of love and peace. Satan incites evil, hatred, deceit, and betrayal.

God allows Satan to test us, therefore!

The book of James says: *"God blesses the people who patiently endure testing. Afterward they will receive the crown of life that God has promised to those who love him. And remember, no one who wants to do wrong should ever say, 'God is tempting me.' God is never tempted to do wrong, and he never tempts anyone else either. Temptation comes from the lure of our own evil desires. These evil desires lead to evil actions, and evil actions lead to death"* (James 1:12–15).

But who gives us these evil desires?

Jesus told the church at Smyrna (Revelation 2:9–10), *"I know about your suffering and your poverty—but you are rich! I know the slander of those opposing you. They say they are Jews, but they really aren't because theirs is a synagogue of Satan. Don't be afraid of what you are about to suffer. The Devil will throw some of you into prison and put you to the test. You will be persecuted for 'ten days.' Remain faithful . . . [unto] death, and I will give you the crown of life."*

About Satan's torment of God's people we read (Zechariah 3:1–2): *"Then the angel showed me Jeshua the high priest standing before the angel of the* LORD. *Satan was there at the angel's right hand, accusing Jeshua of many things. And the*

LORD said to Satan, 'I, the LORD, reject your accusations, Satan. Yes, the LORD, who has chosen Jerusalem, rebukes you. This man is like a burning stick that has been snatched from the fire.'"

This means that Satan loves to point the finger at us. He does this by saying, "Look at what he/she did. I thought he/she was better than that." Or he may openly accuse us of something we did not do. He knows he is telling a lie, but lying is his business.

Lying blinds the eyes of those who look up to us. *"If the Good News we preach is veiled from anyone, it is a sign that they are perishing,"* Paul told us. *"Satan, the god of this evil world, has blinded the minds of those who don't believe, so they are unable to see the glorious light of the Good News that is shining upon them. They don't understand the message we preach about the glory of Christ, who is the exact likeness of God"* (2 Corinthians 4:3–4).

One of the methods Satan employs to blind the minds of God's people is through the messages of his false ministers. They openly tell their people not to listen to what God's ministers are saying. They might say something like this: "He doesn't know what he is talking about, don't listen to him." Or they may openly preach a message designed to undermine the truth about Jesus. Or they may openly preach a message that leads to contention and hostility, instead of peace.

There are many such false ministers around. However, through deceit and cleverness, they are hard to detect. This is what Jesus means by a wolf in sheep's clothing. The wolf speaks and acts as if he is on your side, but his true motive is to "tear your house down." And tear it down, he will.

Satan tried to do this by telling the newly converted Christians that what Paul was preaching about Christ was wrong, and that they needed to return to the Jewish worship system. But Paul was persistent and would not bow to their wishes. The book of Hebrews sums it up like this:

> *The old system in the . . . [Law] of Moses was only a shadow of the things to come, not the reality of the good things Christ has done for us. The sacrifices under the old system were repeated again and again, year after year, but they were never able to provide perfect cleansing for those who came to worship. If they could have provided perfect cleansing, the sacrifices would have stopped, for the worshipers would have been purified once for all time, and their feelings of guilt would have disappeared.*
>
> *But just the opposite happened. Those yearly sacrifices reminded them of their sins year after year. For it is not possible for the blood of bulls and goats to take away sins. That is why Christ, when he came into the world said, "You did not want animal sacrifices and grain offerings. But you have given me a body so that I may obey you. No, you were not pleased*

with animals burned on the altar, or with other offerings for sin. Then I said, 'Look, I have come to do your will, O God—just as it is written about me in the Scriptures'" (Hebrews 10:1–7).

Then in Hebrews 10:9–10 we are told, *"Then he added, 'Look, I have come to do your will.' He cancels the first covenant in order to establish the second. And what God wants is for us to be made holy by the sacrifice of the body of Jesus Christ once for all time."*

Hebrews 7:11–12 adds: *"And finally, if the priesthood of Levi could have achieved God's purposes—and it was that priesthood on which the law was based—why did God need to send a different priest from the line of Melchizedek, instead of from the line of Levi and Aaron?*

"And when the priesthood is changed the law must also be changed to permit it. For the one we are talking about belongs to a different tribe, whose members do not serve at the altar. What I mean is, our Lord came from the tribe of Judah, and Moses never mentioned Judah in connection with the priesthood."

To sum it up, Satan was trying to destroy the Christian religion by lying about it. Lies hurt. Lies turn people against you and your message. Lies make you look like something you are not. Lies cause people to turn against you, where once they were your friends. This is the work of Satan at its best.

Many still will insist that what we have just said is not true. They do this, however, to their own downfall. They fail to see how the blindness of their hearts by Satan leaves them against the very thing that could set them free. They fail to see how Jesus wants us to uplift and not tear down. They fail to see how Jesus wants us to love and not hate. They fail to see how Jesus wants us to look only to Him for salvation, and not look to the things of this world.

Satan is not our friend. Yes, I know people think he is, because they follow him joyfully. They dance to his music, without hesitation. They jump when he calls, as if they have no choice. They do his bidding with all their strength. Yes, they know these things are wrong, but they don't care. All they care about is how it makes them feel, or if they can have success with it, or get away with it.

Then when we ask them to stop their evil ways, they think that we are trying to do them a great disservice. They think that we are trying to make them give up the pleasures they love so much. They say, "We are just having fun and you are trying to stop us." Many of them say, "I have lived this way all of my life. All the people I know live this way, so why would I want to change now?" So they go on doing what they have always done, without any thought of who it hurts, or what anyone thinks about it.

Many Gentiles felt the same way when they first heard the Gospel. The book of Acts tells us:

> *Now there was a believer in Damascus named Ananias. The Lord spoke to him in a vision, calling, "Ananias!"*
>
> *"Yes Lord!" he replied.*
>
> *The Lord said, "Go over to Straight Street, to the house of Judas. When you arrive, ask for Saul of Tarsus. He is praying to me right now. I have shown him a vision of a man named Ananias coming in and laying his hands on him so that he can see again."*
>
> *"But Lord," exclaimed Ananias, "I've heard about the terrible things this man has done to the believers in Jerusalem! And we hear that he is authorized by the leading priest to arrest every believer in Damascus."*
>
> *But the Lord said, "Go and do what I say. For Saul is my chosen instrument to take my message to the Gentiles and to kings as well as to the people of Israel. And I will show him how much he must suffer for me"* (Acts 9:10–16).

But when Paul started to preach the Gospel, the Jews there became very upset. They thought he was trying to make them so something they did not want to do. The Gentiles thought likewise. They did not want to give up their worship of idols or their lustful way of life. Their anger boiled over, and they attacked Paul every chance they got. They accused him of trying to destroy their way of life, the way they had lived for generations.

Paul's response to this was, *"As for me, God forbid that I should boast about anything except the cross of our Lord Jesus Christ. Because of that, my interest in this world died long ago, and the world's interest in me is also long dead. It doesn't make any differences now whether we have been circumcised or not. What counts is whether we really have been changed into new and different people. . . . God's mercy and peace be upon all those who live by this principle. . . ."* (Galatians 6:14–16).

As the abomination of desolation, Satan represents everything that is hateful and distasteful. He leaves his victims empty and void, as if all the hope is taken from them. I know they seem happy, but they are not. They merely move from one bad experience to another. It is as if they are in a cycle that cannot be broken. Or maybe they don't want to break it.

But worst of all, he turns people against the Gospel of Christ. This dooms them to spend their lives in hopelessness and despair and without God in their lives. Such people are lost and on their way to hell. But we must point them to Christ anyway.

Psalm 121 states it this way: *"I look up to the mountains—does my help come from there? My help comes from the* LORD, *who made the heavens and the earth! He will not let you stumble and fall; the one who watches over you will not sleep. Indeed, he who* watches over Israel never tires and never sleeps. The LORD himself watches over you! The LORD stands beside you as your protective shade. The sun will not hurt you by day, nor the moon by night. The LORD keeps you from all evil and preserves your life. The LORD keeps watch over you as you come and go, both now and forever."

But Satan does his best work within the framework of God's church. With all his might, he attempts to tear down the true worship of Jesus, inserting his false worship in its place. This is hard to recognize because he is so clever and charming as he does it. But his intent is to take the place of Christ and have us worship him. Yes, people do this unknowingly, but they still do it.

Satan will be so successful at this as the church age nears its end that the light of the Gospel will be only a flicker. It will almost be wiped out. Jesus spoke of this time like this: *"Immediately . . . [after the tribulation of those days] the sun will be darkened, the moon will not give light, the stars will fall from the sky, and the powers of heaven will be shaken"* (Matthew 24:29).

The sun, the moon, and the stars mentioned by Jesus must be seen as the light of Christ and His Gospel message. In other words, Satan produces smoke that threatens the Gospel itself. It will be as if everything in God's heaven has been shaken. This is how it will be when Christ returns.

Joel 2:30–32 states it like this: *"I will cause wonders in the heavens and on the earth—blood and fire and pillars of smoke. The sun will be turned into darkness, and the moon will turn . . . [blood red] before that great and terrible day of the LORD arrives. Anyone who calls on the name of the LORD will be saved. . . ."*

In Joel 1:1–4 Joel saw the works of Satan and his demons as an invading army of locusts. They ate all the crops and vegetation—symbolic of the "food" of the Gospel being destroyed. These demon locusts spread across the land, making the earth desolate.

"Hear this, you leaders of the people! Everyone listen! In all your history, has anything like this ever happened before? Tell your children about it in the years to come. Pass the awful story down from generation to generation. After the cutting locust finished eating the crops, the swarming locust took what was left! After them came the hopping locust, and then the stripping locust, too!" (Joel 1:2–4).

May God bless those who understand!

17

BLASPHEMY AGAINST THE HOLY SPIRIT

This subject has puzzled church people over the years. They wonder if they have done something or said something that will doom them to hell. The Bible refers to this as blasphemy against the Holy Spirit. The dreadfulness of this possibility places people in needless fear and hopelessness.

I have heard much cursing in my lifetime, but what we are talking about is not this. The subject came up as Jesus healed a demon-possessed man, who was both blind and unable to talk. The crowd was amazed by His power. Some of the people said, *"Could it be that Jesus is the Son of David, the Messiah?"* But the Pharisees, who didn't like Jesus, said, *"No wonder he can cast out demons. He gets his power from Satan, the prince of demons"* (Matthew 12:22–24).

Knowing their thoughts, Jesus said to them, *"Any kingdom at war with itself is doomed. A city or home divided against itself is doomed. And if Satan is casting out Satan, he is fighting against himself. His own kingdom will not survive. And if I am empowered by the prince of demons, what about your own followers? They cast out demons, too, so they will judge you for what you have said. But if I am casting out demons by the Spirit of God, then the Kingdom of God has arrived among you.*

"Let me illustrate this. You can't enter a strong man's house and rob him without first tying him up. Only then can his house be robbed! Anyone who isn't helping me opposes me, and anyone who isn't working with me is actually working against me" (Matthew 12:25–30).

Jesus proceeded to tell them in verses 31–32, *"Every sin or blasphemy can be forgiven—except blasphemy against the Holy Spirit, which can never be forgiven. Anyone who blasphemes against me, the Son of Man, can be forgiven, but blasphemy against the Holy Spirit will never be forgiven, either in this world or in the world to come."*

The common people were not in a position to know that Jesus was the Christ, even though He worked miracles among them. To them He looked just like an ordinary person. For this reason, Jesus was willing to overlook their lack of faith if they repented. But the Pharisees were in a position to know better. They sat in the seat of Moses. They knew the law, i.e., they knew what Moses, the prophets, and the Psalms had written about the coming Christ. However, when Jesus identified Himself to them, they refused to accept Him. The Holy Spirit prompted them to do so, but they blatantly chose to follow Satan, instead (John 8:44). Thus, when they refused to follow the Spirit's leadings, Jesus uttered His famous statement.

It works this way: the Holy Spirit will not force anyone to surrender to the His inclination against his/her own will. He prompts and convicts us, but He will go no further. It is up to the individual to submit. If we prove to God that we will never submit, this seals our fate.

The Pharisees, in their stubborn pride and rebellion, reached this point. As a result, they openly cursed Jesus and the Holy Spirit. This forced God to completely withdraw His Spirit, leaving no other way for them to be saved.

Another way to say this is the Holy Spirit is the only agency God has sent into the world to convict us of sin, and to turn us to the righteousness of Christ (John 16:8). The Pharisees rejected the Holy Spirit's presence by accusing Him of being the power of Satan, and accusing Jesus of working under this power. This forced the Holy Spirit to withdraw Himself from them, with the promise never to return. At this point, their fate was sealed. Now, there was no other means at God's disposal to reach their minds (John 16:8, 13–14). The only influence now left in their lives was that of Satan and his demons.

God help us never to do this ourselves!

The Pharisees, for all intents and purposes, were telling the Holy Spirit that He had no authority on earth to lead anybody to God, and that He belonged in hell. They were also saying that since Jesus was working under Satan's power, He, too, belonged in hell. People, today have a more colorful way of saying it. But this was outright blasphemy, unholy profanity.

The way to control the impulse to curse is to allow the Holy Spirit to rule in our lives (Romans 8:5). Another way is to pray to God on all occasions about the things that trouble us (Ephesians 6:18). Then as many of God's people have experienced, we can began to get rid of all bitterness and rage that leads to cursing and abusive language. Those who follow these principles find that the desire to curse their fellow man is greatly abated and that their feelings of anger are brought under control.

"Don't worry about anything; instead, pray about everything. Tell God what you need, and thank him for all he has done. If you do this, you will experience God's peace, which is far more wonderful than the human mind can understand. His peace will

guard your hearts and minds as you live in Christ Jesus," Paul told us in the book of Philippians.

"And now, dear brothers and sisters [in Christ Jesus], let me say one more thing as I close this letter. Fix your thoughts on what is true and honorable and right. Think about things that are pure and lovely and admirable. Think about things that are excellent and worthy of praise. Keep putting into practice . . . [everything] you learned from me and heard from me and saw me doing, and the God of peace will be with you" (Philippians 4:6–9).

Ephesians 4:25–32 reads:

> *So put away all falsehood and "tell your neighbor the truth" because we belong to each other. And "don't sin by letting anger gain control over you." Don't let the sun go down while you are still angry, for anger gives a mighty foothold to the Devil.*
>
> *If you are a thief, stop stealing. Begin using your hands for honest work, and then give generously to others in need. Don't use foul or abusive language. Let everything you say be good and helpful, so that your words will be an encouragement to those who hear them.*
>
> *And do not bring sorrow to God's Holy Spirit by the way you live. Remember, he is the one who has identified you as his own, guaranteeing that you will be saved on the day of redemption.*
>
> *Get rid of all bitterness, rage, anger, harsh words, and slander, as well as all types of malicious behavior. Instead, be kind to each other, tenderhearted, forgiving one another, just as God through Christ has forgiven you.*

But if we really knew Jesus, we wouldn't want to say evil things about Him. Jesus is the One who delivers us from sin. He did this by dying on a lonely cross on a hill just outside Jerusalem. His death paid for every sin we will ever commit. What better friend can we have?

People don't realize how much Jesus loves us. I don't have the words to properly describe this love. Yes, I can say the words, but they fall far short of my intended meaning. But God's love for us is so great He considered it worth giving His life for. So on an everyday basis; He lets His sun shine on us, even if we have not been good. He lets the rain water our crops. He gives us air to breathe. He gives us good health. He gives us friends to cheer us up on lonely days. He gives us food to eat, water to drink, and the comfort of knowing that we will have this service the next day.

David said this about Jesus: *"You have done many good things for me, Lord, just as you promised. I believe in your commands; now teach me good judgment and knowledge. I used to wander off until you disciplined me; but now I closely follow your word.*

"You are good and do only good; teach me your principles. Arrogant people have made up lies about me, but in truth I obey your commandments with all my heart" (Psalm 119:65).

God help us to heed this advice!

PART 5
BELONGING TO CHRIST

18

THE CHOICE IS OURS: KEEP BELIEVING

Jesus is giving us a choice between life and death. That is, if we choose to follow Him, we will live, but if we do not choose to follow Him, we will not have life. This choice is put forth to us all through the Bible. We must consider it, therefore, and make the right choice so that we can always be with our Savior.

Look at what God said to the people in Jeremiah's time: *"In that day the enemy will break open the graves of the kings and officials of Judah, and the graves of the priests, prophets, and common people. They will dig out their bodies and spread them out on the ground before the sun, moon, and stars—the gods my people loved, served, and worshiped. Their bones will not be gathered up again or buried but will be scattered on the ground like dung. And the people of this evil nation who survive will wish to die rather than live where I will send them. I, the* L ORD *Almighty, have spoken"* (Jeremiah 8:1–3).

Here, God said that people would wish to die. But in the previous chapter, He went into a long discourse about a place called Topheth. Topheth is often used to describe death and hell. See the point.

Jesus said to these same people in Jeremiah 9:11, *"I will make Jerusalem into a heap of ruins. It will be a place haunted by jackals. The towns of Judah will be ghost towns, with no one living in them."* This is a further description of the desolation of hell.

Then to make sure the people really understood, He told them, *"This has happened because my people have abandoned the instructions I gave them; they have refused to obey my law. Instead, they have stubbornly followed their own desires and worshiped the images of Baal . . ."* (Jeremiah 9:13–14).

Jesus expressed it this way in the book of John: *"I assure you, those who listen to my message and believe in God who sent me have eternal life. They will never be* condemned for their sins, but they have already passed from death to life" (John 5:24). He said in Mark 1:15: *"At last the time has come! The Kingdom of God is near! Turn from your sins and believe this Good News. . . . !"*

Those who listen to Jesus' message and those in the kingdom of God are the same people; they are alive because Jesus has given them life!

Matthew 19:23–26 records: *"Then Jesus said to his disciples, 'I tell you the truth, it is very hard for a rich person to get into the Kingdom of Heaven. I say it again—it is easier for a camel to go through the eye of a needle than for a rich person to enter the Kingdom of God!'*

"The disciples were astounded. 'Then who in the world can be saved?' they asked.

"Jesus looked at them intently and said, 'Humanly speaking, it is impossible. But with God everything is possible.'"

Again, only God can give us life and place us in His kingdom. Man, thus, can stop and listen anytime he wants to, but very few of us do. Jesus said in Matthew 13:22 that most people are so concerned with the cares and problems of this present life that the Good News of the life to come is being blocked out.

Other people, today, are like the people of Jeremiah's time. *"We will not listen to your message from the LORD!" they told Jeremiah. "We will do whatever we want. We will burn incense to the Queen of Heaven and sacrifice to her just as much as we like—just as we and our ancestors did before us, and as our kings and princes have always done in the towns of Judah and in the streets of Jerusalem. For in those days we had plenty to eat, and we were well off and had no troubles! But ever since we quit burning incense to the Queen of Heaven and stopped worshiping her, we have been in great trouble and have suffered the effects of war and famine"* (Jeremiah 44:16–18).

They added in verse 19: *"And [really], do you suppose that we were worshiping the Queen of Heaven, pouring out drink offerings to her, and making cakes marked with her image, without our husbands knowing it and helping us? Of course [we were] not!"*

Jesus told us in Luke 18:10–14, *"Two men went to the Temple to pray. One was a Pharisee, and the other was a dishonest tax collector. The proud Pharisee stood by himself and prayed this prayer: 'I thank you, God, that I am not a sinner like everyone else, especially like that tax collector over there! For I never cheat, I don't sin, I don't commit adultery, I fast twice a week, and I give you a tenth of my income.'*

"But the tax collector stood at a distance and dared not even lift his eyes to heaven as he prayed. Instead, he beat his chest in sorrow, saying, 'O God, be merciful to me, for I am a sinner.' I tell you, this sinner, not the Pharisee, returned home justified before God. For the proud will be humbled, but the humble will be honored."

But most people don't take the humble position. They will do or say almost anything to make themselves look good. It seems to be their way of life. Everyone wants people to think well of them. Everyone wants people to think they are something great. They think this is the way to get ahead in life.

And this is so sad. They just do not to believe what Jesus said. In addition, most people do not even want to hear what He said. Our preachers are just as bad.

They won't look in the Bible and read such chapters as Revelation 22 that tells us about the life we will have in heaven because we eat from the TREE OF LIFE, or that we drink from the WATERS OF LIFE. Nor will they look in the same chapter and read where it says that these words are *"trustworthy and true."*

When speaking of preachers who distort the truth, Peter tells us in 2 Peter 2:1–8:

> *But there were also false prophets in Israel, just as there will be false teachers among you. They will cleverly teach their destructive heresies about God and even turn against their Master who brought them. Theirs will be a swift and terrible end.*
>
> *Many will follow their evil teachings and shameful immorality. And because of them, Christ and his true way will be slandered. In their greed they will make up clever lies to get hold of your money. But God condemned them long ago, and their destruction is on the way.*
>
> *For God did not spare even the angels when they sinned; he threw them into hell, in gloomy caves and darkness until the judgment day. And God did not spare the ancient world—except for Noah and his family of seven. Noah warned the world of God's righteous judgment. Then God destroyed the whole world of ungodly people with a vast flood.*
>
> *Later, he turned the cities of Sodom and Gomorrah into heaps of ashes and swept them off the face of the earth. He made them an example of what will happen to ungodly people. But at the same time, God rescued Lot out of Sodom because he was a good man who was sick of all the immorality and wickedness around him. Yes, he was a righteous man who was distressed by the wickedness he saw and heard day after day.*

False messages do not help us!

If we accept the LIFE Jesus offers us, we will be like the five sparrows Jesus talked about in Luke 12:6. They were worth only two pennies to the world, but to God they had great value. Jesus said that *"God does not forget a single one of them."* He goes on to tell us in verse 7, *"And the very hairs on your head are all numbered. So don't be afraid; you are more valuable to him than a whole flock of sparrows."*

He tells us in verses 8–9, *"And I assure you of this: If anyone acknowledges me publicly here on earth, I, the Son of Man, will openly acknowledge that person in the presence of God's angels. But if anyone denies me here on earth, I will deny that person before God's angels."*

We need Jesus, then, to give us life. With this life, we will become one of God's chosen children, destined for heaven and all heaven offers. Heaven will last forever, through all the endless ages. This is so staggering that my mind can't digest it. But it is true.

God saves us because He loves us. Jesus verified this when He told the Samaritan woman, *"If you only knew the gift God has for you and who I am, you would ask me, and I would give you living water. People soon become thirsty again after drinking this water. But the water I give them takes away thirst altogether. It becomes a perpetual spring within them, giving them eternal life"* (John 4:10–14).

Then Jesus told us in John 14:1–4 that He is going to heaven to prepare a place for us to live, and that when the time was right, He will back to get us and take us there:

"Don't be troubled," He said. *"You trust in God, now trust in me. There are many rooms in my father's home, and I am going [there] to prepare a place for you. If this were not so, I would tell you plainly. When everything is ready, I will come and get you, so that you will always be with me where I am. And you know . . . how to get there"* (John 14: 1–4).

John was inspired to write this for us: *"Then a third angel followed them, shouting, 'Anyone who worships the beast and his statue or who accepts his mark on the forehead or the hand must drink the wine of God's wrath. . . . Let this encourage God's holy people to endure persecution patiently and remain firm to the end, obeying his commands and trusting in Jesus.'*

"And I heard a voice from heaven saying, '[This you] write . . . down: Blessed are those who die in the Lord from now own. Yes, says the Spirit, they are blessed indeed, for they will rest from all their toils and trials; for their good deeds follow them!'" (Revelation 14:9–13).

The eternal life offered to us by Jesus is too valuable to reject. I plead with every unsaved person who reads this message to accept Jesus as your Savior. JESUS IS THE ONLY WAY, THE ONLY TRUTH, AND THE ONLY LIFE. Please choose Jesus, today, and live forever!

Choosing Jesus is not easy in this sinful world, though. Distractions are everywhere. You may not know this, but this world is under Satan's administration. Yes, God is its owner and maker, but still, God allows Satan to deceive us, tempt us, torment us, and cause us to sin. And, wow, he has done his job well.

Paul told us (1 Timothy 6:12–14), *"Fight the good fight for what we believe. Hold tightly to the eternal life that God has given you, which you have confessed so well before many witnesses. And I command you before God, who gives life to all, and before Christ Jesus, who gave a good testimony before Pontius Pilate, that you obey his commands with all purity. Then no one can find fault with you from now until our Lord Jesus Christ returns."*

We must fight with all our might. Even when we think we are losing, we must fight. We must fight when everyone tells us to give up. The race is not won by those who quit along the way. They may have started out strong and heard the cheers of those standing along the sideline. But if they quit, everything is lost. We must be strong and run all the way to the end. This is real faith.

When emphasizing the importance of our faith, Paul tells us in the book of Romans, *"I want you to know . . . that I planned many times to visit you, but I was prevented until now. I want to work among you and see good result, just as I have done among other Gentiles. For I have a great sense of obligation to people in our culture and to people in other cultures, to the educated and uneducated alike. So I am eager to come to you in Rome, too, to preach God's Good News.*

"[Amen] . . . I am not ashamed of this Good News about Christ. It is the power of God at work, saving everyone who believes—Jews first and also Gentiles. This Good News tells us how God makes us right in his sight. This is accomplished from start to finish by faith. As the Scriptures say, 'It is through faith that a righteous person . . . [is given] life'" (Romans 1:13–17).

We could say it like this: God does not make us His children in a vacuum. Specifically, He will not save us without a corresponding show of faith on our part. Otherwise, He would not know whether salvation is what we really want, or just something He has forced on us. In this way, He avoids the problem of us saying later that He made us do something we really did not want to do (Romans 1:18–32). If we remember correctly, Satan was placed in heaven without any corresponding show of faith on his part, and we can see what happened in his case (Ezekiel 28:11–19).

This is how we can have complete assurance that we are saved. We must put our trust (faith) in Christ and keep it there until the end of our lives. By this, I mean that we must put our trust in God by believing what He says about Christ and His salvation. Then, we must not let anything stop us from believing.

The point is: Jesus is our God and Savior. This means He is the only way we can overcome this evil world and gain life. Why would anyone reject Him? All that is left is eternal death in hell. That's not too good.

The famous hymn, "I Have Decided to Follow Jesus," attributed to S. Sundar Singh, states our situation perfectly:

> I have decided to follow Jesus;
> I have decided to follow Jesus;
> I have decided to follow Jesus;
> No turning back, no turning back.

Though I may wonder, I still will follow;
Though I may wonder, I still will follow;
Though I may wonder, I still will follow;
No turning back, no turning back.
The world behind me, the cross before me;
The world behind me, the cross before me;
The world behind me, the cross before me;
No turning back, no turning back.
Though none go with me, still I will follow;
Though none go with me, still I will follow;
Though none go with me, still I will follow;
Though none go with me, still I will follow;
No turning back, no turning back.
Will you decide now to follow Jesus?
Will you decide now to follow Jesus?
Will you decide now to follow Jesus?
No turning back, no turning back.[1]

Let's conclude this discussion like this: as we continue to believe, God has promised to continue to save us. And we know that God's word is trustworthy and true. So put your faith in Jesus and believe everything He has told us.

BLESS THE LORD!

---

1 S. Sundar Singh, "I Have Decided to Follow Jesus," available from, <http://library.timelesstruths.org/music/I_Have_Decided_to_Follow_Jesus/>.;Internet; accessed 14 October 2011, p 1.

19

THE RAPTURE

Many Christians teach a doctrine they refer to as the Rapture. Then they go on to explain that the second coming of Christ is divided into two phases, one phase before the tribulation and the other phase after the tribulation. The Rapture, thus, is the first phase. But this is not true. It leads to the belief that there are two second comings, instead of one, as Christians have traditionally believed.

But Jesus never said that He was coming back twice. He always spoke of His coming as the end of the world. And if it is the end, then it is the end; there can't be a later coming. Besides, what will we do if some Bible scholar starts to speak of a third coming?

As for me, I only began to take notice of this theory the late 1980s. At this time, I heard preachers talking about it as if it were really going to happen. Then they talked about what would happen afterward, that is, the tribulation and the millennial reign of Christ.

One Scripture people use to support this theory is 2 Peter 3:10: *"But the day of the Lord will come as unexpectedly as a thief . . ."* (2 Peter 3:10). This may suggest a secret event. However, there's more. The last part of this verse says, *". . . Then the heavens will pass away with a terrible noise, and everything in them will disappear in fire, and the earth and everything on it will be exposed to judgment."* They place special emphasis on the words "unexpectedly as a thief." Jesus, however, makes no reference to this as the first of two comings, nor does Paul in his writing about this event. And neither should we!

Let's look at what the Luke says about Christ's return.

Acts 1:6–11 records:

When the apostles were with Jesus, they kept asking him, "Lord, are you going to free Israel now and restore our kingdom?"

"The Father sets those dates," he replied, "and they are not for you to know. But when the Holy Spirit has come upon you, you will receive power and will tell people about me everywhere—in Jerusalem, throughout Judea, in Samaria, and to the ends of the earth."

It was not long after he said this that he was taken up into the sky while they were watching, and he disappeared into a cloud. As they were straining their eyes to see him, two white-robed men suddenly stood there among them. They said, "Men of Galilee, why are you standing here staring at the sky? Jesus has been taken away from you into heaven. And someday, just as you saw him go, he will return!"

Did you catch that? The angels said that Jesus would return "just as you saw him go." And not in some "secret" manner! In other words, the return of Jesus will be visible to everyone. So why do we see all this confusion?

I believe this is a trick by Satan to take our minds off Jesus, and His salvation, and place them on things we don't need to worry about. The theories, however, are endless. One group says one thing, and other groups say something else. How can a new Christian know who is right? Some groups say the Rapture will take place before the tribulation, some say it will take place during the tribulation, and others say it will take place afterwards.

If we believe what Jesus and Paul taught, and what the early Christians believed, we wouldn't have this confusion!

Matthew 24:29–31 says, *"Immediately after . . . [the tribulation of those days], the sun will be darkened, the moon will not give light, the stars will fall from the sky, and the powers of heaven will be shaken. And then at last, the sign of the coming of the Son of Man will appear in the heavens, and there will be deep mourning among all the nations of the earth. And they will see the Son of Man arrive on the clouds of heaven with power and great glory.*

"And he will send forth his angels with the sound of a mighty trumpet blast, and they will gather together his chosen ones from the farthest ends of the earth and heaven."

Notice! This occurs "immediately after" the tribulation, not before. It also says, "then at last." This means there is no coming of Christ before this event or after this event! It makes no mention of a thousand-year reign after this event either.

Jesus continues (verses 36–42): *"However, no one knows the day or the hour when these things will happen, not even the angels in heaven or the Son . . . Only the Father knows.*

"When the Son of Man returns, it will be like it was in Noah's day. In those days before the Flood, the people were enjoying banquets and parties and weddings right up to the time Noah entered his boat. People didn't realize what was going to happen until the Flood came and swept them all away. That is the way it will be when the Son of Man comes.

"Two men will be working together in the field; one will be taken, the other left. Two women will be grinding flour at the mill; one will be taken, the other left. So be prepared, because you don't know what day your Lord is coming."

If "no one knows the day or the hour" and "you don't know what day your Lord is coming," then the second coming can't be seven years after the Rapture, as many claim. If so, we would know the exact day or hour Jesus would return!

Matthew 13:47–50 says, *"Again, the Kingdom of Heaven is like . . . [the] fishing net that is thrown into the water and gathers fish of every kind. When the net is full, they drag it up onto the shore, sit down, sort the good fish into crates, and throw the bad ones away. This is the way it will be at the end of the world. The angels will come and separate the wicked people from the godly, throwing the wicked into the fire. There will be weeping and gnashing of teeth."*

Notice that the separation of the good from the bad happens at the very end of time, not before! This is further proof that there will be only one end-time appearance of Christ.

Some additional Scriptures that support the Bible's position are listed below:

- *"And one of the four living beings handed each of the seven angels a gold bowl filled with the terrible wrath of God, who lives forever and forever. The Temple was filled with smoke from God's glory and power. No one could enter the Temple until the seven angels had completed pouring out the seven plagues"* (Revelation 15:7-8). Did you catch that? No one was all allowed to enter the Temple, a symbol of heaven, until the seven plagues had past.
- *"When the world hates you, remember it hated me before it hated you. . . . Since they persecuted me, naturally they will persecute you . . ."* (John 15:18–20). The persecution (tribulation) against Jesus was very great, and so will it be against us.
- *"Shadrach, Meshach, and Abednego replied, 'O Nebuchadnezzar, we do not need to defend ourselves before you. If we are thrown into the blazing furnace, the God whom we serve is able to save us. . . . But . . . if he doesn't . . . be sure that we will never serve your gods or worship the gold statue you have set up'"* (Daniel 3:16–18). God allowed these three brave men

to be thrown into this furnace as a picture and type of what He will allow us to go through.

But most disturbing of all, the Rapture theory does away with the need for Jesus to take us to heaven. Why would Jesus allow us to stay in heaven for seven years, only to bring us back to the earth? Remember that some saints have been in heaven for hundreds of years. Others have been there for only a short time. But the church has traditionally taught that all will be in heaven forever. I prefer to believe the traditional teaching.

The Bible position, then, is that the return of Jesus will be a single event, a single event to call home the saints and to wrap up world events.

The RAPTURE, often called "The blessed hope," is sadly, a false doctrine. It leads us to believe in a distorted view of end-time events. But we cannot neglect our responsibility to prove the truth. But I am sad to say that many people will not find the moral courage to do this. They will, then, continue in their false "hope," and suffer great disappointment when Christ finally does return. I only hope that you will not be one of them.

May the Lord bless you and keep you!

20

GOD IS SPIRIT

Jesus said to the Samaritan woman, *"But the time is coming and is already here when true worshipers will worship the Father in spirit and in truth. The Father is looking for anyone who will worship him that way. For God is Spirit, so those who worship him must worship in spirit and in truth"* (John 4:23–24). But what is spirit? Better yet, exactly what is spirit composed of?

First, let's look at what the Bible says. Philippians 2:5–8 (KJV) tells us that if we are saved, we have the mind of God. *"Let this mind be in you, which was also in Christ Jesus. . . ."* 1 Corinthians 2:12 (NIV) tells us that we have the Spirit of God. *"We have not received the spirit of the world but the Spirit who is from God, that we may understand what God has freely given us."* In these Scriptures, the words *spirit* and *mind* are synonymous. They have the same meaning.

In addition, we read in Romans 12:1–2 (KJV) that we should be renewed in our minds. Then, in Romans 8:14, we are told we should let God lead our spirits. And we are told in Romans 8:16 (KJV) that God's Spirit bears witness with our spirit. This is further proof these words mean the same thing.

In reference to the minds/spirits of man, Luke 6:8 (KJV) reads, *". . . he knew their thoughts, and said to the man. . . ."* Let's translate it this way: ". . . He knew what their minds or spirits were thinking, and said to the man. . . ."

The same is true of God when we speak of Him as a Spirit. God is pure Spirit or pure Mind. Another way to say it is God is pure Intellect or Consciousness. In other words, He is not flesh and blood with a body. Nothing exists but His undiluted Mind or Spirit. This makes God a pure Spirit or Mind who thinks. But God does speak of Himself as having hands, feet, a face, etc. He does this in the metaphoric sense, however. That is, He does this to relate to us.

But let's get back to God as pure Spirit or Mind. Romans 5:5 (KJV) reads: *"And hope maketh not ashamed; because the love of God is shed abroad in our hearts by the Holy Ghost which is given unto us."* Psalms 51:11 (KJV) reads: *"Cast me not away from thy presence; and take not thy Holy Spirit from me."* Do you see the point? Here God's presence is equated with His Spirit!

Psalm 51:10 (KJV) compares the heart to the spirit: *"Create in me a clean heart, O God; and renew a right spirit within me."*

This means that we can't escape from God's spirit. David said in Psalm 139:7–12: *"I can never escape from your spirit! I can never get away from your presence! If I go up to heaven, you are there; if I go down to the place of the dead, you are there. If I ride the wings of the morning, if I dwell by the farthest oceans, even there your hand will guide me . . . your strength will support me.*

"I could ask the darkness to hide me and the light around me to become night— but even in darkness I cannot hide from you. To you the night shines as bright as day. Darkness and light are both alike to you."

Jeremiah 23:21–24 states: *"'I have not sent these prophets, yet they claim to speak for me. I have given them no message, yet they prophesy. If they had listened to me, they would have spoken my words and turned my people from their evil ways. Am I a God who is only in one place?' asks the* LORD. *'Do they think I cannot see what they are doing? Can anyone hide from me? Am I not everywhere in all the heavens and earth?' asks the* LORD.*"*

God *can* localize His presence! This is how God was seen walking with Adam in the garden. He appeared to Abraham and Moses this way. His most impressive localization was when He appeared in human flesh. Localization does not mean that God is limited, however. He is still the all-present God, driving the universe.

Let's say it this way. While God was on earth in His human body, He was still the all-present God that we read about in the Old Testament. This is one of His greatest miracles. It baffles the mind. But it is true. Think about it like this: if God was not holding the universe together, who was?

Knowing all of this will do us no good if we don't understand how much God loves us. 1 John 3:1 tells us: *"See how much our heavenly Father loves us, for he allows us to be called His children, and we really are!"*

That God calls us His children is the greatest compliment He can give us. Too many human fathers don't look upon the ones they brought into the world this way. Some children are neglected, others are estranged, and some are outright discarded by their parents. This leaves them empty and hopeless. They wonder if anyone loves them. Something inside of me tells me that if I could just express to them that somebody cared, it would make all the difference in the world.

Somebody does care, though. His name is Jesus. He loves us more than we will ever know. But without the preaching of the Gospel, most people never know this. That's why we should spread the love of Jesus every chance we get.

The verse continues: *"But the people who belong to this world don't know God, so they don't understand that we are his children."*

This makes me understand why the early Christians had so much trouble. The people around them thought they were strange. Just think about it. Here were people giving allegiance to a strange new God called Jesus. Nobody had ever heard of Him. All they knew was their pagan gods—the gods of thunder, storms, wind, air, etc. These gods didn't show any love or affection to them. If you displeased them, they would bring disaster upon you. As a result, they spent a great deal of time making appeasements.

This is why people are often mean to us. They just don't have the love of Jesus in their hearts. They may say they do, but they don't. Others get upset or openly hostile when you remind them of this. Some resort to even more hostility. Some just turn and walk away.

But Jesus is not like this. He openly tells us He loves us. In fact, love is His dominant quality. That's why the Bible says that God is Love. This love is displayed to us all the time, we just don't think about it. In fact, if God stopped loving us for one second, we would go out of existence.

Jesus was nice to everyone He met. He fed them when they were hungry. On one occasion, He fed five thousand men at one time. On another occasion, He fed four thousand. He healed people when they were sick. And He didn't even ask for anything in return. How many people do we know like this?

But His greatest act of love was giving Himself over to death in our place. Who would do this but Jesus?

John continues in 1 John 4:12: *"Dear friends, since God loved us that much, we surely ought to love each other."*

Love for others is placed in us by God's Spirit. If it is not, then no matter how hard we try, our love for others will not be manifested. We must ask Jesus for this kind of love. And He will give it to us. He is just waiting for us to ask. We can just say, "Lord Jesus, I am having trouble loving this person, please help me."

Verse 12 reads: *"No one has ever seen God. But if we love each other, God lives in us, and his love is brought to full expression through us."*

But didn't John see Jesus when He was on earth? Yes he did! What John is talking about is that no one has seen God in His spirit essence. And we haven't. As we said above, all we have seen is God's localizations. But the point is, when we love others, people are able to see God's love in action. And this lets them know that God is near.

This verifies the facts that God loved us before we loved Him. Because as humans, we don't know what love is. We don't see love expressed in nature. Only the strongest survive in nature. The weak has hardly any chance to live. We see very little love in politics or business. Never in sports do we see love. The aim in sports is to get the best of your opponent, not to help him win. But God is not like this; He wants us to win.

This is why He has promised to give us bodies just like the glorified body of Jesus. Just think of it; we will not want for anything and have no fears or doubts. We will live forever with the One who loves us and be His friends.

David speaks of God's love in Psalm 91:1–2: *"Those who live in the shelter of the Most High will find rest in the shadow of the Almighty. This I declare of the LORD; He alone is my refuge, my place of safety; He is my God, and I [trust] . . . him."*

This means that the love of Jesus acts like a giant shadow; it covers all who stands in it. This is most comforting in times of stress and trouble. That is, just to know that Jesus is watching us and is near us gives us peace. I am not saying that He has to remove the trouble; oftentimes He doesn't. But still, just to know that He cares is sometimes all we need.

God is our refuge because He protects us from danger and things that may harm us!

He goes on to say that God will rescue us from every trap. God will protect us from the fatal plague. God will shelter us with His wings. God will protect us from the terrors of the night and God will protect us from the dangers of the day. But these types are evidenced spiritually in the fact that no sins will be counted against us when we stand before Him on the Day of Judgment. Then in heaven, we will sin no more. GOD, HASTEN THE DAY!

May God, who alone is wise, be with you forever through our Lord Jesus Christ!

EPILOGUE

A FINAL WORD TO THE CHURCH

Jesus is the personality around who our Christian religion revolves. And if we don't preach about Jesus, our religion will not have a solid foundation. When the storms come, and the rain falls, and the wind blows, our house will fall. God help us not to be like this. Listen to what is recorded about Jesus:

"Then the Lord *told Abram, 'Leave your country, your relatives, and your father's house . . . go to the land I will show you. I will cause you to become the father of a great nation. I will bless you and make you famous, and I will make you a blessing to others.*

"I will bless those who bless you and curse those who curse you. All the families of the earth will be blessed through you" (Genesis 12:1–3).

This prophecy was fulfilled in Jesus a descendant of Abraham!

We are told in Isaiah 11:10–11 that Jesus would be the banner of our salvation: *"In that day the heir to David's throne will be a banner of salvation to . . . the world. The nations will rally to him, for the land where he lives will be a glorious place. In that day the* Lord *will bring back a remnant of his people for the second time, returning them to the land of Israel. . . ."*

This was fulfilled when Jesus commissioned the Gospel to be preached to the world.

Malachi 4:2–6 says this about Jesus: *"'[Truly,] . . . for you who fear my name, the Sun of Righteousness will rise with healing in his wings. And you will go free, leaping with joy like calves let out to pasture. On that day when I act, you will tread upon the wicked as if they were dust under your feet,' says the* Lord *Almighty.*

"Remember to obey the instructions of my servant Moses, all the laws and regulations that I gave him on Mount Sinai for all Israel.

"Look, I am sending you the prophet Elijah before the great and dreadful day of

the LORD *arrives. His preaching will turn the hearts of parents to their children, and the hearts of children to their parents. Otherwise I will come and strike the land with a curse.'"*

This was fulfilled when John told us about Jesus' coming and pointed Him out to the crowds.

However, sadly enough, when Jesus appeared on the scene, many of His own people (the Jews) did not know who He was! And even worse, they didn't want His sacrificial atonement for them.

Luke 4:14–30 states it this way:

> *Then Jesus returned to Galilee, filled with the Holy Spirit's power. Soon he became well known throughout the surrounding country. He taught in their synagogues and was praised by everyone....*
>
> *All who were there [then] spoke well of him and were amazed by the gracious words that fell from his lips. "How can this be?" they asked. "Isn't this Joseph's son?"*
>
> *Then he said, "Probably you will quote me that proverb, 'Physician, heal yourself'—meaning, 'Why don't you do miracles here in your hometown like those you did in Capernaum?" But ... no prophet is accepted in his own hometown....*
>
> *When they heard this, the people in the synagogue were furious. Jumping up, they mobbed him and took him to the edge of the hill on which the city was built. They intended to push him over the cliff, but he slipped away through the crowd and left them.*

But to all of us who receive Christ, He is the Light of our darkened path. *"The LORD is my light and my salvation—so why should I be afraid? The LORD protects me from danger—so why should I tremble?*

"When evil people come to destroy me, when my enemies and foes attack me, they will stumble and fall. Though a mighty army surrounds me, my heart will know no fear. Even if they attack me, I will remain confident," Psalm 27:1–3 tells us.

My hope and plea is that all the unsaved who read this book will come to Christ and be saved. And under the inspiration of the Holy Spirit, we have given you the pure and true Gospel message. So accept Jesus now by praying this prayer:

"Lord, please save me, for I am a sinner. Cleanse me from all my sins and make me yours."

Amen!

ABOUT THE AUTHORS

The Reverend W. Lewis Autrey was born in Luverne, Alabama, in 1942. His father, Reverend W. C. Autrey (deceased, 1989), taught him about Christ as soon as he was old enough to comprehend the meaning of the word. His mother, Ellie Mae Autrey, reinforced this teaching with frequent Bible studies and prayer services.

Reverend Autrey met his wife, Joyce E. Autrey, in the fall of 1960 where both were students at Tuskegee University, Tuskegee, Alabama. They were married June 10, 1965. Three children, April L. Autrey, Lewis C. Autrey, and Robert S. Autrey, were born to this union.

In addition to serving in the military as a First Lieutenant, Reverend Autrey has worked as a school teacher, bank manager, salesman, and in the advertising field. Currently he serves as a frequent guest speaker at a prominent South Florida Nursing Home.

Robert S. Autrey is the son of Reverend W. Lewis Autrey. He earned a BS degree in social work from Alabama State University. In 2006, he was called to preach and has been active in the study of God's Word ever since.

God has given this father and son a message to deliver to His Church. It is a message concerning the identity of God Himself—that God speaks to us through His second person, Jesus Christ.; that by the death of Jesus Christ, God redeems (rescues) man from the present state of death he brought upon himself by his sin in the garden; and that Jesus will return and take us to heaven!

You may contact Rev. Autrey at
good_shepard_baptist_church@yahoo.com
or Good Shepard Baptist Church
4429 SE 50th Avenue
Okeechobee, Florida 34974

www.ingramcontent.com/pod-product-compliance
Lightning Source LLC
Chambersburg PA
CBHW032358040426
42451CB00006B/54